# THE ANCIEN RÉGIME

C. B. A. BEHRENS

THAMES AND HUDSON · LONDON

PRINTED IN GREAT BRITAIN BY JARROLD AND SONS LTD NORWICH

ISBN 0 500 32006 3 CLOTHBOUND
ISBN 0 500 33006 9 PAPERBOUND

# CONTENTS

# PREFACE

A book of 40,000 words on the Ancien Régime by an English historian calls for an apology. A foreigner who tries to generalize about the affairs of other nations is always exposed to pitfalls. In this case they seem particularly numerous and I cannot hope to have avoided them. Their presence is nevertheless my excuse for writing this essay. The study of the Ancien Régime is peculiarly bedevilled by a great mass of learned monographs on the one hand and, on the other, by the lack of any general works that make the subject intelligible to English readers. In these circumstances it seems that an explanation that is coherent, and to the best of the writer's ability takes the relevant facts into account, is better, whatever errors it may be held to contain, than no explanation at all.

The attempt to explain so much in so small a space may have led to a degree of compression that the general run of readers will find troublesome. An apology may be due on this account too, though with the qualification that it was in response to the general reader's known desire for brevity that the publishers imposed the word limit. The glossary has been devised to remedy this inconvenience as far as possible.

The writer owes many debts of gratitude – some to people who prefer to remain anonymous, some to Cambridge University and Newnham College (whose ways of proceeding have made certain aspects of the Ancien Régime intelligible which otherwise might not have been so), some, particularly, to Mr Stanley Baron of Thames and Hudson for his unfailing patience.

NE POUR LA PEINE

Reueille matin de Campagne

But des gens de Campagne Tailles payee

L'ABEILLE ou la mouche à miel
Chacun a part à ses trauaux

LA VACHE

par son moyen l'on boit et mange

LE COCHON
Il est meprisé et necessaire

LA POULE
sa journée est d'un petit prix

# I INTRODUCTION
## THE NATURE OF THE ANCIEN RÉGIME

The term Ancien Régime is most commonly applied to the way of life and government in France which the Revolution destroyed. As such, it may seem merely a label attached to certain social and political arrangements which plainly came to an end in 1789, but about whose beginnings and distinguishing characteristics there is no agreement. Any book on the subject must start by considering what these distinguishing characteristics were, within what period of time they manifested themselves, and whether or not they were peculiar to France, since it is now often held that the Ancien Régime was a European and not merely a French phenomenon.

These questions are ones that are not usually asked because the French Revolution was so momentous an event that attention has always been focused on its causes and consequences; the régime which it destroyed has seemed interesting only as a prelude to it and not as a phenomenon in its own right. This was Tocqueville's point of view. The title of his famous work is *l'Ancien Régime et la Révolution*, and he summed up his purpose in writing it in his last chapter, which he entitled 'how the Revolution emerged of itself out of the conditions which preceded it'.

Because it has been judged by the standards of the age that succeeded it and in the light of the revolutionary propaganda, the Ancien Régime has seemed to be distinguished principally by its abuses, and the date of its origins has been fixed at whatever moment the historians concerned with it have assumed that the more significant abuses took root. To some, this moment has seemed to be the very beginning of absolute monarchy. In the series of French textbooks called *Que Sais-je*, for example, the work entitled *l'Ancien Régime* covers the period 1500 to 1789. To others, the trouble appears to have started not with absolutism in its early stages or in its prime but in its period of decline. Cherest, whose *Chute de*

9

◀ 1 'Born to suffer'. Eighteenth-century cartoon of the French peasant

*l'Ancien Régime* is still the last full-scale study of the subject, though he wrote it in 1884, began his account in 1715. To the revolutionaries, on the other hand, the Ancien Régime began with feudalism, which the National Assembly, in the words of the famous decree of 4 August 1789, declared that it had 'totally abolished'.

This question of dates is important since the essential characteristics of any régime will be judged differently if the régime itself is differently delimited. Our opinions on the nature of the Ancien Régime must vary according to whether we assume that it came into existence in the ninth century or the sixteenth or the eighteenth. We cannot profitably begin to discuss it until we can assign approximate dates to it. But how are we to assign it dates, even approximately, unless we have some idea of what its distinguishing characteristics were?

An examination of the meaning of the term itself can help us to escape from this dilemma. It was first used in the 1790s by people who meant by it what we mean today when we use the same or similar words to describe any order of things which has been superseded because of revolutionary changes. One does not speak of an old régime except with reference to the new régime which has replaced it. Implicit in the term is thus the idea of decay. On the other hand, a new régime, even if it comes in by revolution, never involves a complete break with the past, and an old régime goes under only after a period in which it has failed to work because it has been subject to tensions out of which the new order is born. By definition, one might say, any old régime is a régime distinguished by conflict between old and new practices and attitudes.

There is much evidence to prove that educated French people, in the decades before the Revolution, believed that their régime was of this kind. As Voltaire once said, we 'live in curious times and amid astonishing contrasts: reason on the one hand, the most absurd fanaticism on the other . . . a civil war in every soul. *Sauve qui peut.*'[1] When Voltaire contrasted reason and fanaticism he was making a distinction that was a commonplace in his generation. By fanaticism he meant essentially a belief, impervious to argument, in the rightness of existing prejudices and practices (particularly those of the

2 Gabriel Sénac de Meilhan (1736–1803), son of one of Louis XV's physicians, *Intendant* of Hainault (1775), frequenter of the *salons* and writer of some repute, who after the outbreak of the Revolution repudiated the ideas of the Enlightenment in favour of those of the 1660s

Roman Catholic Church); by reason he meant essentially a willingness to consider new practices and ideas on their merits. When he said that there was a civil war in every soul he meant that every French person, or at least every reflecting French person, was torn between attachment to the old order and the awareness that it would no longer work.

The contrasts and conflicts in the realm of ideas, to which Voltaire referred, are commonly seen by French historians as a reflection of contrasts and conflicts in the realm of material facts due to the impact of money, earned in commerce, industry and finance, on a customary society in which prestige was based on land, on birth, and on privilege, in the sense of special rights guaranteed by law to particular persons and groups. This opinion, too, was a commonplace at the time. Every ambitious author felt that he had to write on the theme which Sénac de Meilhan chose in 1787 in order to prove his qualifications for the post of finance minister – which, in the event, went to Necker. Sénac de Meilhan called his work *Considerations sur les richesses et le luxe*, and chose this title because of the popularity of the

3 The growing deficit of the treasury is the subject of this satire showing Louis XVI and Necker (in fact Calonne in the original version) apparently astounded before the empty coffers, while an aristocrat and a priest (Loménie de Brienne, *see Ill. 104*) make off with sacks of money

subject. Money earned in industry, commerce and finance, it was continually said, disrupted the old relationships – relationships between peasant and *seigneur*, between bourgeois and nobleman, among noblemen themselves – and widened the gap between rich and poor. Its distorting effects seemed epitomized in the contrasts between town and country – between the wealth in the towns and the poverty in the countryside, familiar to the readers of Arthur Young, who after spending a night in Nantes in the autumn of 1788 was moved to exclaim: 'Mon Dieu!... do all the wastes, the deserts, the heath, ling, furze, broom and bog that I have passed for 300 miles lead to this spectacle? What a miracle, that all this splendour and wealth of the cities of France should be so unconnected with the country! There are no gentle transitions from ease to comfort, from comfort to wealth; you pass at once from beggary to profusion, from misery in mud cabins to Mademoiselle Saint-Huberty, in splendid spectacles at 500 livres a night.'[2]

This phenomenon, however, and the others which it was held to symbolize, were not peculiar to the eighteenth century. They had

12

4 The port of Marseille in 1754

been features of French life and subjects of criticism for at least a century and a half before the Revolution. Admittedly for various reasons, and particularly because of a great expansion in the colonial trades, commerce and industry increased at a faster rate than previously between the beginning of the 1730s and the end of the 1770s. Even in this period, however, the pace could not be described as revolutionary. It was, in fact, far too slow to absorb the great increase in population, which rose from some 19 million in 1715 to some 26 million in 1789. By 1789 the proportion of the population that lived in towns of over 2000 inhabitants has been estimated at only 15 per cent. The process by which the customary, hierarchical society was eroded by social and economic change was, in fact, a very slow one and a long way from completion when the Revolution broke out. It has no significant landmarks. Landmarks only emerged when the cumulative effects of the erosion combined with other causes to produce new attitudes of mind.

There seems to have been some consensus among contemporaries that this happened around the end of the 1740s. The historian

13

Rulhière, for example, in a speech to the French Academy in 1787, said that the year 1749 was the one 'in which a general revolution in manners and letters began'.[3] The diarist Barbier was of the same opinion. The author of the article 'Epargne', in the first edition of the *Encyclopaedia*, thought that the year 1748 had seen a revolution in the attitude to economic questions; Louis XV's chancellor, Maupeou, in describing the growth of opposition to the Crown among the Parlements, said that it was 'particularly since 1750 that they have shown themselves more menacing and better organized'.[4]

It was during the middle years of the century, in fact, that established beliefs and practices first came under widespread attack. Hitherto, the abuses in social and political life had been condemned as departures from the principles on which the old order rested. Now 'reason' was summoned to challenge 'fanaticism' and the principles themselves were called in question.

Thus there emerged a revolutionary ideology. The people responsible for it, however, were not revolutionaries but were all members or associates of the ruling class, and hammered out their ideas in the Paris *salons*. Starting from certain common assumptions, they nevertheless differed, and were content to differ, widely in their conclusions. They produced no revolutionary party, nor a political party of any kind. Their ideas did not constitute a coherent body of doctrine but, on the contrary, were often mutually incompatible. For this reason, however, they appealed to many different classes of people, who found in them support for different aspirations and chose from among them those that suited their purposes. They evoked their strongest response from ministers and officials; on the other hand, they provided a justification for individual and collective acts of defiance against authority, committed on behalf of different interests and justified on different grounds, until by the 1780s, as the Comte de Ségur expressed it: 'From one end of the kingdom to the other opposition became a point of honour. It seemed a duty to distinguished minds, a virtue to the generous, a weapon useful to the Philosophes in their struggle for liberty: in fact a way of distinguishing oneself and a fashion which all youth adopted with ardour.'[5]

14

5 Benjamin Franklin, United States ambassador to France, 1776–85, and hero of the Paris *salons*, is the subject of this allegory by Fragonard. The Latin legend reads: 'He has snatched from the sky its thunder and from tyrants their sceptres' ▶

If one asks what set this train of events in motion, one can hardly fail to be struck by the coincidence that the years which saw the beginnings of this revolution in beliefs and in attitudes to authority were also the years which saw the conclusion of the War of the Austrian Succession by the Treaty of Aix-la-Chapelle in 1748, and the consequent attempts of the French government to adjust its domestic policies to the facts of defeat. These policies, though they fell so far short of their aim that the French experienced far more disastrous defeats between 1756 and 1763, had painful consequences for most of the population. Particularly, it was not possible to lighten the burden of direct taxation after the end of the war. It had always been known to fall too heavily on the peasants; after 1748 it had to be increased and the nobility were also subjected to it. The year 1749 was the first when French noblemen were required to pay direct taxes (and at a rate in effect much higher than that imposed on their English counterparts), not to meet a war emergency but as a permanent, peace-time measure.

6 The anchorage of Toulon, the principal naval base of France, 1755

The war of which these events were the consequence, was itself a concomitant of the process of social and economic change which France was undergoing in the eighteenth century, since colonial expansion involved fighting the British. The struggle between France and Britain had begun in 1689 and went on until 1815. It was concerned essentially with two issues which to contemporaries, and rightly, always seemed interrelated: on the one hand, hegemony in Europe; on the other, sea-power and control over the trades with India, West Africa, the West Indies and North America. At the accession of William III it was the British who had seen themselves in danger of destruction, not only as a commercial power, but as a Protestant power, and a power ruled by a parliamentary monarchy. By the middle of the eighteenth century, however, their religion, their form of government and their maritime ascendancy were all beyond the strength of France to jeopardize. Now it was the French themselves whose power in Europe and overseas was in jeopardy. By 1740, when the War of the Austrian Succession started, the

French had already abandoned the claim to world hegemony, for which Louis XIV and Colbert had striven. The war itself seemed to demonstrate that even hegemony in Europe was permanently beyond their reach. By 1748 the British were not only supreme at sea; by mobilizing the resources of the New World to redress the balance of the Old, they had acquired the determining voice in deciding the frontiers of the European belligerents.

In such circumstances, attention in France was naturally directed to the causes of this change of fortunes. This stimulated comparisons between the social and political order in Britain, which had attained its military objectives, and that in France, which had not. The contrast impressed on both the government and the ruling class the urgent need for reform. It was thus far from an accident that the social and political ideas of the Enlightenment began to gain general currency around 1748. Owing their philosophical, social and political inspiration in the first place to British thinkers and the British example, and with roots going back in France at least to the time of Louis XIV, these ideas began to have a wide appeal after the middle of the century because of the answer they seemed to provide to the prevailing discontents.

It is thus possible to discern, around 1748, the emergence of a particular conjunction of circumstances: a degree of social, economic and demographic change sufficient in itself to create tensions, but greatly exacerbated by a burden of taxation much too heavy in total and extremely inequitably distributed; a consciousness of national inadequacy, manifesting itself in continual comparisons between France and Britain to the former's detriment; the crystallization of grievances in a revolutionary ideology, which condemned the whole order of things in church, state and society, but produced no programme of action. The propounders and apostles of the new ideas, however hopeful some of them might be of change in the distant future, saw little hope of it in the immediate one. The gap between their aspirations and the existing state of affairs was one they could see no means of bridging, except by the intervention of some *deus ex machina*, such as Rousseau's legislator. When the Philosophes were asked to give their advice on practical matters (and they were

7  An assembly of Philosophes: Voltaire (1), d'Alembert (4), Condorcet (5) and Diderot (6)

often consulted by foreign governments), they invariably showed themselves to be conservative. Thus, in spite of the social and political tensions, and the revolutionary nature of the opinions in general circulation, there was no body of people before late into the 1780s who could conceive of revolution. It was this contempt for the old values, combined with unawareness of the implications of the new, that gave the last decades before 1789 its *fin de siècle* atmosphere. Speaking of the group of radical young nobles, the friends and collaborators of the Philosophes, to which he himself belonged, Ségur said that they walked 'on a carpet of flowers that concealed from us the abyss'.[6]

8 *Salon* life. In this sketch by François Boucher of Mme Geoffrin's famous *salon*, the actor Lekain is reading Voltaire's *Orphelin de la Chine* before a bust of the then exiled author

If these are the characteristics of the Ancien Régime in France, then the applicability of the term to the rest of Europe in the second half of the eighteenth century must seem dubious. Admittedly many of the characteristics of French ways of life and thinking between 1748 and 1789 also prevailed elsewhere. When the Vicomte de Valmont, in *Les Liaisons Dangereuses*, for example, feared that he might make France too hot to hold him he said that he would go abroad: 'Does one not live abroad just as one does here?' All the states of Christian Europe at the end of the eighteenth century were, like France, agrarian communities, dominated by hereditary aristocracies. Many were also ruled by absolute monarchs. In all of them, sometimes for reasons unconnected with events in France and sometimes because of conscious imitation, the existing social order became, to a greater or lesser extent, an object of criticism. Professor Palmer has familiarized us with the idea that the whole of what he calls Atlantic civilization – that is, the civilization of all the countries bordering on the western and eastern seaboards of the North Atlantic – 'was swept in the last four decades of the eighteenth century by a single revolutionary movement, which manifested itself in different ways and with varying success in different countries, yet in all of them showed similar objectives and principles'.[7] No one would dispute this. The question is, however, whether the similarities between France and these other countries were more significant than the differences. There is a strong case for saying that they were not. Though many individual characteristics of French life and thought were also to be found elsewhere, the combination of characteristics that distinguished the Ancien Régime in France was not only unique, but without close parallels at the time. In proof of this, it is only necessary to point out that no nation except the French experienced a major social revolution in the eighteenth century.

There could be no close parallel between France and the minor powers, not only because the domestic arrangements in these smaller States were to a greater or lesser extent at the mercy of their more powerful neighbours, but because they were not subject to the same degree, if they were subject at all, to the burden imposed by the need to maintain large armaments. As Professor Palmer shows, by the middle of the eighteenth century French civilization and English civilization resembled each other sufficiently to make comparisons possible. The British, however, had executed one king, exiled another, and as a result established parliamentary government in the course of the seventeenth century. Thereafter, the most sinister features of French civilization did not exist in England. A rapidly rising population and a more or less static agriculture; a crushing burden of taxation, the weight of which tended to increase with the poverty of the tax-payer; an arbitrary absolutism; a society privileged in the particular sense already described and suffering from the diseases of defeat – these characteristics, particularly, of the French social and political scene were absent from the English. In the remaining major powers, on the other hand (that is, Prussia, Russia and the Habsburg dominions), many of them existed in a more pronounced form, but nevertheless provoked little open complaint.

There can be no revolution, Lenin once said, without a revolutionary theory; but this presupposes groups that are educated as well as discontented. Outside France at the end of the eighteenth century no such groups existed in any major continental country. In the militarized and regimented society of Prussia no one criticized the existing social and political arrangements until these were called in question by the successes of the French revolutionary armies. In the hereditary lands of the house of Habsburg, though there was discontent, the level of political sophistication was even lower than in Prussia. In Russia a considerable proportion even of the nobility was still illiterate. Among the leading powers in the second half of the eighteenth century, it can thus be said, a major social revolution was possible only in France, since in England there was not the same cause for it, and in the other powers no substantial body of educated opinion in favour of it.

If one wishes to find parallels to the situation in France between 1748 and 1789, one must look for them not in western Europe at that time, but in central and eastern Europe in later times. Even so, the parallels will be inexact, not only because every historical situation is unique, but because the Revolution altered everyone's attitude to reform. By alarming the conservatively-minded on the one hand, and, on the other, by inspiring the radicals with the knowledge that major social revolutions were a possibility for which one could plan, it precluded that alliance between the propounders of revolutionary ideas and the leaders of the aristocracy which had been a distinguishing feature of the French Enlightenment. With these qualifications, however, it is possible to discern, in central and eastern Europe at different dates in the nineteenth century, the same phenomena which distinguished France in the eighteenth: a backward peasant economy and an advancing urban one, which nevertheless did not advance fast enough to absorb the growing population; a society privileged in the same sense in which the French was privileged; an arbitrary absolutism losing its self-confidence and authority because of military defeat and a decline in national power; the development of a body of revolutionary ideas. Such a conjunction of circumstances existed in Prussia. for example, in the decades that preceded and followed the collapse in 1806, and in Russia at the end of the century.

In these circumstances, though one must admit that the Ancien Régime was not a phenomenon peculiar to France, one must also admit that it was one which some nations can be said never to have experienced (since in their cases the changes were too gradual), and that those which did experience it experienced it at different periods. If this is so, and since the reason for affixing labels is to make plain differences and identities, no point can be served by applying the term to Europe at any moment in the eighteenth century, except in the sphere of international relations. Here, however, it serves a purpose.

In the history of international relations, the year 1789 was a landmark, as it was in French history, and so also was 1748. Just as the French, in the second half of the eighteenth century, commonly contrasted their own age with that of Louis XIV, so the elder Pitt, in the famous speech he made in the Commons in December 1762, on the preliminaries to the Peace of Paris, contrasted the European situation of Louis XIV's day with that which had emerged after the Treaty of Aix-la-Chapelle. He pointed to what he called the 'extinguishing' of Holland as a major military power and to the rise of Prussia and Russia; to the relative increase in British and the relative decline in French strength; to the changes in the alliances and alignments in Europe that had resulted from these facts. 'Such', he concluded, 'are the great events by which the balance of power in Europe has been entirely altered since the grand alliance'[8] against Louis XIV.

In European, as in French history, the years 1748 to 1789 form a unity distinguished by a combination of circumstances that was unique. This was the period when the balance of power, from having been an article of faith, became an apparently irreversible fact. Frederick the Great pointed out that all the four major powers of Europe – the French, the Austrians, the Russians and the Prussians – maintained armies of comparable size, efficiency and equipment. 'The most that princes can expect', he said, 'from a succession of military victories is some little town on the frontiers, or some suburb

... whose population is greatly inferior to the numbers ... who have perished in the campaigns.'[9] Whatever might happen in the world overseas (and these were the years in which the American colonies won their independence), in the internal history of Europe, as in that of France, it seemed that nothing could change.

This state of affairs, however, was maintained largely because of conditions inside France and the nature of French foreign policy. That the French possessed enough resources to upset the equilibrium on the Continent is proved by the achievements of the Revolution and Napoleon, which were not accompanied by increased production or technical inventions, but were due simply to the more effective mobilization of resources for use in land warfare. That the French government failed to establish the hegemony for the sake of which it entered the war in Europe in 1741, and that it afterwards had to abandon the attempt, was due partly to the amount of effort it put into the war at sea with Britain, and partly to its inability to lay its hands on men, supplies and weapons to the extent that proved possible after the Revolution. Thus when the Ancien Régime fell in France (and with it the naval tradition, so that the navy was first crippled and then destroyed and war at sea became impracticable), it brought down with it the European state system in which the French had played a principal part.

These facts dictate the theme of this book. It cannot attempt to describe the Ancien Régime as it manifested itself at different dates in different European countries. It can only be concerned with the first manifestation, which as such, nevertheless, might be held to be the most important. Its purpose is to consider the Ancien Régime in France between 1748 and 1789 in the setting of the European events, and the struggles among the European nations for trade and colonies, which played an important part in its history, as it did in theirs.

# II THE INHERITANCE AND THE HEIRS

In every country in Europe in the eighteenth century, the vast majority of people earned their living from the land. In France the category commonly described as peasants – that is, everyone who was not a nobleman, a cleric, or engaged full-time in some occupation other than agriculture – must have included by 1789 some 22 or more million souls out of a total population reckoned at 26 million.

The civilization on which the eighteenth century prided itself was the prerogative of only a very small minority, even in France, where the educated were more numerous than in most other countries. For the vast majority, life was a continual, and often a losing, battle to wring a bare livelihood from the soil. The calculations of governments and of private individuals revolved round the harvest. In France in the eighteenth century, the Contrôle Général (the department responsible for financial and economic affairs) issued every year to each of four hundred local officials a form divided into columns – one for wheat, one for rye, one for oats, etc. – with instructions to note the amounts that were harvested in the current year and that remained over from the previous harvest. In the words of Professor Labrousse: 'the problem of grain dominated all the other problems'.[1]

Bad harvests, though the substantial landowners and merchants benefited from the rising prices, meant shortage if not starvation for most people, in town and country alike; for most people, in France as in the greater part of the rest of Europe, either owned no land, or owned an amount insufficient to support a family, or worked land belonging to other people on terms that, for the most part, barely sufficed to meet their needs even when times were good.

The price of bread (and of wine in the wine-growing areas) was always the determining factor in the economy. As it rose in times of scarcity it diminished the amount that the poor could spend on other things. Consequently, agricultural calamities had repercussions on the urban and rural industries, which gave employment in the towns and supplemented that in the countryside, and whose products the majority in town and country could only afford when the price of bread was low or moderate.

Bad harvests also had repercussions on the government's revenues, since the yield of the taxes fell, and on its projects for moving about and provisioning its armies. In addition, they created administrative difficulties, since people who are starving have various ways of making themselves a nuisance to the authorities. Throughout the greater part of Europe in the eighteenth century peasant revolts were endemic. In some of the countries of central and eastern Europe – in Bohemia in 1772, in Russia during the Pugachev revolt of the following year – there were times when they reached the proportions of civil war. They had done so in France in the reign of Louis XIV, but this did not happen again until the spring of 1789, partly, no doubt, because there was no general famine, but partly also, it has been suggested, because the royal administration became more efficient. Scarcity nevertheless remained common, and hunger the fear and experience of most people. In bad times in France the unemployed and starving would band together and roam the countryside in search of food. They would attack the wagons carrying the grain to market and break into the barns where it was stored. Illiterate and brutalized by misery, the victims of irrational fears and superstitions which, if the strong hand of authority were removed, could set whole districts on the march against the scapegoats of the moment, they were always a potential menace to law, order and property, even in France where, if Ségur may be believed (and the facts seem to support him), they were normally more docile, and less hostile to the landlords, than in the serf-owning countries of Prussia, Russia and the Habsburg dominions.

In these circumstances, no government could be indifferent to the fate of the peasants, and none, the French government included, in principle ever was. Self-interest and Christian morality alike preached the same lesson: that the peasant had to be helped as far as possible in

26

9 Table regulating the price of bread, drawn up at Le Mans in 1715 ▶

# TABLE
# POUR LES BOULANGERS
## DE LA VILLE DU MANS,

SERVANT d'Instruction pour sçavoir le prix du Pain, à raison de la valeur du Bled,
conformement à l'Arrêt de la Cour du 19. Iuin 1638. en consequence de l'Essay qui en
a été fait ès Années mil six cens trente-trois & mil six cens trente-quatre.

LE PRIX DU PAIN BLANC, Sera imposé sur le prix & à raison de quarante-deux Douzaines de Petit Pain Blanc du poids de huit onces par Charge de Froment, qui sera exploitée par les Boulangers de cette Ville du Mans, ausquels avons taxé la somme de quarante huit sols pour leurs salaires, impenses & droit de Commerce, d'exploiter châcune Charge de Bled Froment, en outre le profit du Rebelut qui leur demeurera, sans que le prix du Pain puisse hausser ou diminuer, sinon que la Charge de Bled Froment hausse ou diminué du moins de quarante sols, à laquelle raison.

LORSQUE la Charge de Bled Froment vaudra dix livres d'achapt, y ajoûtant ladite somme de quarante huit sols pour les frais & salaires : Ledit Pain blanc du pois de huit onces vaudra six deniers. Le Grand Pain blanc de seize onces, douze deniers.

| A douze Livres la Charge de Bled Froment. | A dix huit Livres la Charge de Bled Froment. | A vingt-quatre Livres la Charge de Bled Froment. |
|---|---|---|
| Le petit Pain blanc de huit onces, vaudra sept deniers. | Le petit Pain blanc de huit onces, vaudra dix deniers. | Le petit Pain blanc de huit onces, vaudra treize deniers. |
| Le Grand Pain blanc de seize onces, quatorze deniers. | Le Grand Pain blanc de seize onces, vingt deniers. | Le Grand Pain blanc de seize onces, deux sols deux deniers. |

| A quatorze Livres la Charge de Bled Froment. | A vingt Livres la Charge de Bled Froment. | A vingt-six Livres la Charge de Bled Froment. |
|---|---|---|
| Le petit Pain blanc de huit onces, vaudra huit deniers. | Le petit Pain blanc de huit onces, vaudra onze deniers. | Le petit Pain blanc de huit onces, vaudra quatorze deniers. |
| Le Grand Pain blanc de seize onces, seize deniers. | Le Grand Pain blanc de seize onces, vingt-deux deniers. | Le Grand Pain blanc de seize onces, deux sols quatre deniers. |

| A seize Livres la Charge de Bled Froment. | A vingt-deux Livres la Charge de Bled Froment. | |
|---|---|---|
| Le petit Pain blanc de huit onces, vaudra neuf deniers. | Le petit Pain blanc de huit onces, vaudra douze deniers. | |
| Le Grand Pain blanc de seize onces, dix-huit deniers. | Le Grand Pain blanc de seize onces, deux sols. | |

ET ainsi en ascendant lorsque la Charge de Bled Froment haussera de quarante sols, le petit Pain blanc de huit onces haussera toûjours d'un denier; Et le Grand Pain blanc de seize onces haussera de deux deniers, & baissera aussi à la même raison.

ET pour le regard du Pain bis, le prix y sera aussi imposé à raison de trente-six Pains de châcun douze Livres pesant par Charge de Bled Seigle, qui sera aussi exploitée par lesdits Boulangers, ausquels avons taxé la somme de trente sols pour leurs salaires, impenses & droit de Commerce outre le prix du son qui leur demeurera, sans que le prix dudit Pain puisse être haussé ou diminué, sinon que la Charge de Seigle hausse ou diminué du moins de vingt sols : A laquelle raison.

LORSQUE la Charge de Bled Seigle vaudra huit livres d'achapt, y ajoûtant ladite somme de trente sols pour Droit de Cuisse & Commerce, le Grand Pain de douze livres, vaudra cinq sols quatre deniers : Celui de six livres, deux sols huit deniers : Celui de quatre livres, vingt-deux deniers : Et celui de deux livres, onze deniers.

| A neuf Livres la Charge de Bled Seigle. | A treize Livres la Charge de Bled Seigle. | A dix-sept Livres la Charge de Bled Seigle. |
|---|---|---|
| Le Pain de douze livres, vaudra cinq sols dix deniers. | Le Pain de douze livres, vaudra huit sols un denier. | Le Pain de douze livres, vaudra dix sols quatre deniers. |
| Le Pain de six livres, deux sols onze deniers. | Le Pain de six livres, quatre sols. | Le Pain de six livres, cinq sols deux deniers. |
| Le Pain de quatre livres, deux sols. | Le Pain de quatre livres, deux sols huit deniers. | Le Pain de quatre livres, trois sols cinq deniers. |
| Le Pain de deux livres, douze deniers. | Le Pain de deux livres, seize deniers. | Le Pain de deux livres, vingt deniers. |

| A dix Livres la Charge de Bled Seigle. | A quatorze Livres la Charge de Bled Seigle. | A dix-huit Livres la Charge de Bled Seigle. |
|---|---|---|
| Le Pain de douze livres, vaudra six sols cinq deniers. | Le Pain de douze livres, vaudra huit sols sept deniers. | Le Pain de douze livres, vaudra dix sols dix deniers. |
| Le Pain de six livres, trois sols trois deniers. | Le Pain de six livres, quatre sols trois deniers. | Le Pain de six livres, cinq sols cinq deniers. |
| Le Pain de quatre livres, deux sols deux deniers. | Le Pain de quatre livres, deux sols dix deniers. | Le Pain de quatre livres, trois sols sept deniers. |
| Le Pain de deux livres, treize deniers. | Le Pain de deux livres, dix-sept deniers. | Le Pain de deux livres, vingt-deux deniers. |

| A onze Livres la Charge de Bled Seigle. | A quinze Livres la Charge de Bled Seigle. | A dix-neuf Livres la Charge de Bled Seigle. |
|---|---|---|
| Le Pain de douze livres, vaudra sept sols. | Le Pain de douze livres, vaudra neuf sols deux deniers. | Le Pain de douze livres, vaudra onze sols cinq deniers. |
| Le Pain de six livres, trois sols six deniers. | Le Pain de six livres, quatre sols sept deniers. | Le Pain de six livres, cinq sols neuf deniers. |
| Le Pain de quatre livres, deux sols quatre deniers. | Le Pain de quatre livres, trois sols un denier. | Le Pain de quatre livres, trois sols dix deniers. |
| Le Pain de deux livres, quatorze deniers. | Le Pain de deux livres, dix-huit deniers. | Le Pain de deux livres, vingt-trois deniers. |

| A douze Livres la Charge de Bled Seigle. | A seize Livres la Charge de Bled Seigle. | A vingt Livres la Charge de Bled Seigle. |
|---|---|---|
| Le Pain de douze livres, vaudra sept sols six deniers. | Le Pain de douze livres, vaudra neuf sols neuf deniers. | Le Pain de douze livres, vaudra douze sols. |
| Le Pain de six livres, trois sols neuf deniers. | Le Pain de six livres, quatre sols onze deniers. | Le Pain de six livres, six sols. |
| Le Pain de quatre livres, deux sols six deniers. | Le Pain de quatre livres, trois sols trois deniers. | Le Pain de quatre livres, quatre sols. |
| Le Pain de deux livres, quinze deniers. | Le Pain de deux livres, dix-neuf deniers. | Le Pain de deux livres, deux sols. |

ET ainsi en ascendant, lorsque la Charge de Bled Seigle haussera de vingt sols : Le Pain de douze livres haussera toûjours de sept deniers, & les autres Pains à proportion : Comme à semblable, lorsque la Charge de Bled diminuéra de vingt sols, le prix du Pain baissera à la même raison.

NOUS oüy le Procureur du Roy : ordonnons que le contenu ci-dessus sera Gravé en une Table d'Attain, & mis en la Chambre du Conseil de ce Siege, pour y avoir recours quand besoin sera, à la diligence de Guillaume Senais, Gilles Gasnet, & Antoine Lasne Maîtres jurez Boulangers. Donné au Mans pardevant Nous Antoine Pousset, Conseiller du Roy, Bailly Prevôt & Juge ordinaire, Civil, Criminel & de Police de la Prevôté, Ville & Quinte dudit Lieu, le huitième jour d'Avril mil six cens quarante-un.

Signez,          POUSSET,      Et      GALLOIS.

AU MANS, Chez Loüis Peguineau, Imprimeur à l'Enfant-Jesus, 1715.

10 The king as the father of his people. This cartoon from the famine year of 1709 shows bread being distributed from the Louvre to such of the starving millions as the royal bounty could reach

times of natural calamity; that he had to be protected against exploitation by the landlords; that he should not be subjected to unduly heavy taxation; above all, that the government should rigidly control the grain trade and maintain buffer stocks, in order to mitigate the effects of bad harvests and their attendant troubles.

Between the ideals of the paternalistic monarchies and the treatment the peasant received in practice, however, there was always a large gap, since the monarchs continually found themselves forced or tempted into pursuing policies contrary to the peasants' interests, and were unable or unwilling to prevent their officials and other classes of the population from doing the same. Until the days of the Enlightenment, and indeed often afterwards, the absolute monarchs were given to the pursuit of glory by means of war and conspicuous consumption. Louis XIV built great palaces, kept a splendid court, and – at vastly greater expense – maintained an army that, at its peak,

11　View of Versailles in 1722

is said to have numbered a million men, of whom one-third were
mercenaries but who still had to be paid and fed. This was a larger
army than the French ever raised again before the present century,
and in Louis' long period of personal rule, which lasted for fifty-five
years, war, after the first seven, was almost continuous. The enormous
cost of his military operations inevitably fell, for the greater part, on
the bulk of the population which consisted of peasants.

In the reign of Louis XIV, the peasant thus paid heavily for the
glory of his king and country, and he continued to do so throughout
the eighteenth century. Apart, however, from the prestige of
belonging to a great nation (which there is no reason to suppose he
appreciated), the sums of which he was mulcted brought him in no
return, even in the long run, since they contributed nothing to the
productivity of the land from which he lived and did much to
diminish his own incentive to increase it.

Since the days of Colbert, the French government, like most other governments, had always been aware that its war potential turned on the sums it could raise in taxes and that these, in their turn, were largely dependent on the amount of wealth to be taxed. The way to increase a nation's wealth, however, had seemed to be to increase its shipping and foreign trade, particularly the colonial trades, and its industries as a means to trade. The example of the Dutch had greatly fostered this point of view. In the seventeenth century they had achieved a degree of power internationally that was wholly disproportionate to their numbers – in 1700 their population was only about 2 million – and they owed this to their wealth, which had enabled them to maintain a large army of mercenaries and the greatest navy and merchant fleet in the world. Their wealth, however, had been built up principally on their fishing, their merchant ships and their trade. By the time of Louis XIV's death, the British were supplanting the Dutch as the largest shipowning and naval power, and their experience seemed to point the same moral, which was reinforced by the experience of private individuals. Great fortunes did not come from the profits of agriculture. When they were not accumulated from the perquisites of office or the manipulation of the royal revenues, they came principally from commerce, in particular the expanding commerce with the colonies. The spectacular successes achieved by these means inspired successive French governments with the conviction that commerce and colonies were essential to national greatness. As Choiseul, then Louis XV's minister, said in 1759, France could no longer be considered a first-class power because the British in that year had destroyed the French navy, conquered the French colonies and driven French merchant ships off the seas. These facts, Choiseul concluded, showed that the rank of a first-class power could belong only to a nation that 'possessed the empire of the sea'.[2]

While, therefore, the French government was not indifferent to the fate of the peasants, it nevertheless always subordinated the needs of agriculture, in the short term, to the needs of war, and in the long term, to the needs of trade and industry as it understood them. Colbert had recruited skilled workers from other countries by means

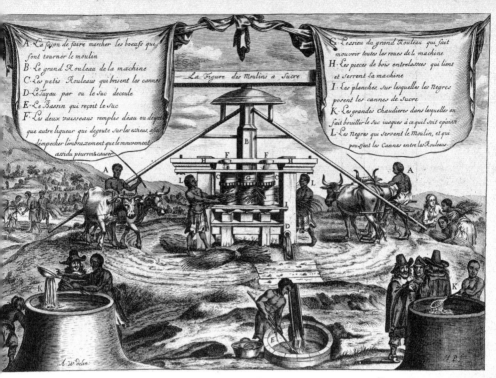

A · La façon de faire marcher les boeufs qui font tourner le moulin
B · Le grand Rouleau de la machine
C · Les petis Rouleaux qui brisent les cannes
D · Le tuyau par ou le Suc decoule
E · Le Bassin qui reçoit le Suc
F · Les deux vaisseaux remplis d'eau ou de quelque autre liqueur qui degoute sur les essieux afin d'empecher l'embrazement que le mouvement assidu pourroit causer

La Figure des Moulins a Sucre

G · L'essieu du grand Rouleau qui fait mouvoir toutes les roues de la machine
H · Les pieces de bois entrelassees qui lient et serrent la machine
I · Les planches sur lesquelles les negres posent les cannes de Sucre
K · Les grandes chaudieres dans lesquelles on fait bouillir le Suc iusques à ce qu'il soit epaissi
L · Les Negres qui servent le Moulin, et qui poussent les Cannes entre les Rouleaux

12 Colonial industry: engraving of a sugar mill in St Dominique (Antilles)

of tax concessions and other benefits. In his day and on various occasions afterwards, the French government had sunk large sums in founding, developing and maintaining its colonies (tasks which in Britain were left to private enterprise), as well as in providing for their defence. It gave subsidies to merchants and manufacturers, whom it also virtually exempted from direct taxation, because, as in other countries until the turn of the eighteenth century (England included), the administration was incapable of assessing, even approximately, incomes derived from any source except land, and the arbitrary taxation of commercial wealth, it was feared, might kill the goose that laid the golden eggs. The government recouped itself by imposing heavy taxes on the sale of articles of general consumption, particularly wine and salt, and by laying the burden of direct taxes on the land.

31

The royal taxes hung like a millstone round the peasant's neck (and also, contrary to what is generally believed, round the necks of most noble landowners). The proportion of the peasant's means of livelihood that was taken from him in direct taxes varied so greatly from one part of France to another, and from one category of peasants to another, that no general estimate of it is possible. It is nevertheless significant that Turgot, when he was *Intendant* in the Limousin, attempted to estimate it in 1766 in relation to the peasant proprietors in two districts for which he could find sufficient data, and concluded – as a result of several different methods of calculation, all of which he claimed yielded comparable results – that these proprietors were paying from 50 to 60 per cent of the gross value of their produce in direct taxation (that is, the value of the produce before deduction had been made for seed, which Professor Labrousse estimates required in general from a quarter to a fifth of the harvest). Turgot was a meticulous writer, and on this occasion was engaged in an official correspondence, with every reason to be accurate. His estimate is likely to be as good as any. Its purpose was to prove that the province for which he was responsible was much more heavily taxed than some others in the more prosperous regions of north-western France – the so-called *pays de grande culture*, where the land was mainly let to tenant-farmers. He did not, however, believe that taxation was generally much lighter in the remaining four-sevenths of France where, as in the Limousin, share-cropping prevailed.

No peasant was exempt from the direct taxes unless, being wholly destitute, he had nothing to give, and their destructive effects were greatly increased by the ways in which they were assessed and collected. In France, as in most other absolute monarchies, it was impossible to induce the monarchs to relate their projects to their resources. For this reason, and because of the administrative difficulties, the direct taxes were never adjusted to the capacity of the tax-payers. The principal direct tax, the *Taille*, which fell only on the peasants, was imposed as a lump sum on the provinces (apart from certain provinces with special privileges), and was then divided up among the parishes where the responsibility for paying it was collective. If the collectors failed to raise the stipulated sums, or absconded with

13 The peasant's dream. Engraving of 1789 showing a peasant who has managed to buy a donkey and is consigning it to hell with a load of tax-collectors

the money, the richest inhabitants had to make good the difference, until Turgot caused the law to be amended in 1775. Not surprisingly, this destructive provision, as Turgot described it, gave every peasant of substance the incentive to leave the village for the town. It was rare, Tocqueville said, to find more than one generation of rich peasants in the villages.

Whether the royal taxes were heavier in the eighteenth century than they had been in the reign of Louis XIV is a question which people at the time and later often debated. Tocqueville believed that they were, because new taxes, or analogous impositions such as the *corvée* (that is, forced labour without payment on the roads), were continually added to the existing ones. No attempt has been made to assemble the data which might make a judgement possible. Because of a combination of causes, however, among which one must give taxation an important place, the French did not invest capital in the

33

modernization of their agriculture as the English did. The English had begun in the seventeenth century to embark on those agricultural improvements which were to astonish the world in the 1760s – the enclosures; the experiments with new crops and new implements; above all, 'the *combination* of animal and arable husbandry',[3] which on the one hand made more manure available, thus increasing the yield of the land and diminishing the need to leave it fallow, and on the other hand, by means of root crops and better pasture, made it possible to improve the quality and augment the number of animals.

The prerequisite of these achievements, however, was the abolition of the communal system of agriculture and of the so-called *servitudes collectives* (the obligation on all landholders to plant the same crops and sow and harvest at the same time), in favour of individual ownership. The individual's strips of land, scattered over the open fields, had to be consolidated and enclosed. In France in the eighteenth century, for reasons that must be discussed later, it proved impossible to make significant headway with this task. What was known as *vaine pâture*, the right of all the inhabitants of the village, the *seigneur* included, to pasture their beasts on the common fields after the harvest, precluded the enclosures which were the prerequisite of the new agriculture. Most of France, in consequence, continued to remain imprisoned in what was known to French agronomists in the eighteenth century as the 'infernal circle' of the fallow land. Because so large an amount of land was always fallow, as much as possible of the rest had to be put under grain. This meant a shortage of pasture and, in turn, a shortage of animals. A shortage of animals, however, meant a shortage of manure; and the shortage of manure made the fallow seem imperative.

This state of affairs condemned the bulk of even the nobility to poverty by the English standards of the time. It would be contrary to common sense to assume that (apart from the small number of people with very large estates or access to sources of wealth other than agriculture) the noble landowners could have dissociated their fortunes from the fortunes of the cultivators of the land. Towards the end of the Ancien Régime this indeed became a platitude in enlightened circles. In Turgot's words, 'When the post-horse falls

34

14 Agriculture. Ploughing. This engraving from the *Encyclopaedia* shows the preoccupation of Diderot and his contributors with the useful arts and crafts, particularly in agriculture, and with the technical inventions of the age, such as Jethro Tull's plough, shown in fig. 2 ▶

fig. 5

fig. 6

fig. 7

fig. 1

fig. 4

fig. 3

fig. 2

Defehet et Prevost Fec.t

*Agriculture, Labourage.*

down from exhaustion, the rider falls also, though the horse is more to be pitied.'[4]

It is commonly implied by French historians that the privileged orders were principally to blame for the peasants' condition, and that the taxes imposed on peasants by the church and the nobility were as great as, if not greater than, those imposed by the state. Proverbially it is the last straw that breaks the camel's back, and in this sense the impression may be justified. It is hardly so in any other. The church took its *dîme*, or tithe, levying it on the gross product of the harvest on all land, whether belonging to peasant, bourgeois or nobleman. It seemed a heavy imposition, but it was not usually as much as a tenth and thus lighter than in England. The *seigneurs* took their feudal dues. These, however, were as much a consequence as a cause of the general poverty.

15 The peasants pay homage to their *seigneur* during his feast. The original caption reads, 'May we enjoy our happiness for many years to come'

16, 17 The peasant problem as explained by the Revolutionary propaganda in 1789: peasants carrying the clergy and nobility on their backs

When the National Assembly put an end to these dues on 4 August 1789 it declared that in so doing it had 'totally abolished the feudal régime'. In fact, as is generally agreed, by that time the relations of peasant and *seigneur* were in many respects no longer feudal, however feudalism is understood. In France in the eighteenth century, the *seigneur*, or lord of the manor, did not, as in central and eastern Europe, work his land himself with serf labour. As in England, he let out all except what he needed for his own use to tenants with whom he concluded a commercial bargain, though these tenants, unlike the English, were for the greater part not tenant-farmers but *métayers* or share-croppers. His feudal dues were rights which the law allowed him, in accordance with the principle of *nulle terre sans seigneur*, over land which was to this extent dependent on him – in his *mouvance*, as it was called at the time – but which was not in any other respect his property.

37

18 Rural industry: plate from the section *Oeconomie Rustique* of the *Encyclopaedia*

In the terminology of the eighteenth century, which has continued in use ever since, it was land which the peasant was said to 'own', and in total it is generally thought to have accounted by 1789 for about 35 per cent of the cultivated land of France (some 20 per cent of the rest being owned by the nobility, some 30 per cent by the bourgeoisie on the outskirts of the towns, and most of what remained by the church). These so-called peasant proprietors, being very numerous, owned plots usually too small to support a family, so that they were forced to supplement their means of livelihood in other ways: for example, by share-cropping. Indeed, the plots were often so small that the term proprietor, when applied to their possessors, must seem a mockery. It was, nevertheless, the current term, and was justified in the sense that the peasant so described could not be evicted from his land, and could sell, bequeath or mortgage it as he saw fit. He was, however, subjected, as for that matter the *seigneur* was himself (for ownership in the modern sense was unknown in the countryside), to the *servitudes collectives* and to feudal dues.

The dues which the peasant proprietor paid to the *seigneur* were in part analogous to a money rent, which was generally very small. Sometimes, though much more rarely, they included payments in kind, which could be heavy. Usually they imposed on the peasant obligations such as to grind his corn in the *seigneur's* mill, to bake his bread in the *seigneur's* oven, to allow the *seigneur* special grazing rights and rights to hunt over his land.

It was obligations of this kind that were principally objected to. They were a constant source of damage, annoyance and frustration, and increasingly resented, as many *seigneurs* (though what proportion of the total we do not know) took to leasing them out to agents who had an interest in enforcing the letter of the law and an eye to claims that had been allowed to lapse.

It was, nevertheless, continually pointed out that the *seigneurs* did not derive a material benefit from their dues at all proportionate to

19 Engraving from the *Encyclopaedia*, to illustrate the article on 'Feudal dues', demonstrating the *seigneur's* hunting rights

the harm or the bitterness they caused. This was the theme of a famous work, written by a certain Boncerf, and called *Les inconvénients des droits féodaux*, which was published in 1776. Boncerf maintained that the mediocre sums which the dues on an average brought in were eaten up by the costs of enforcing them, of keeping the records, and of financing the interminable lawsuits to which they gave rise, which descended from father to son, and which, as he said, 'devour the *seigneurs*, the vassals and the land'. There seems no reason to doubt that, in general, this was true. On the rare occasions when the profits of commercial agriculture were large enough to drive the point home, there were landowners who saw the sense in Boncerf's thesis and allowed their dues to lapse. Public opinion among the *seigneurs*, however, in general remained in favour of them because, as is usual in poor agrarian societies, tradition, prestige and power over other human beings were valued more highly than material progress.

To be a *seigneur* was a great thing, and the dues were a symbol of authority. So it had always seemed to the rich bourgeois, who, for generations before the Revolution, had bought *seigneuries* for this reason, and also because their possession, after a lapse of time, conferred a prescriptive right of entry into the nobility. So it seemed, too, to the established aristocrats. Money was not everything, as Chateaubriand's father thought, in common with the rest of his class. Coming from a distinguished but impoverished family, he re-habilitated the family fortunes by entering the shipping business. He had a share in various merchant ships that plied between France and the West Indies during the War of the Austrian Succession and the Seven Years War, when most of such ships were driven off the seas. In these circumstances, freight rates could rise to astronomical heights and M. de Chateaubriand evidently benefited from them. He appears to have been a person of considerable business skill. Nevertheless, when he bought back the family estates, as his son tells us in his *Memoires d'Outre-tombe*, his proud and authoritarian temperament found its greatest satisfaction in the meticulous exaction of his dues.

When Arthur Young, in his travels, once met a peasant woman, whom he discovered to be twenty-eight years old though she had the appearance of sixty or seventy, she exclaimed to him : 'Les tailles et les droits nous écrasent.'[5] This cry has echoed down the centuries, repeated by one generation of historians after another, who have usually assumed, as the peasant woman doubtless did herself, that the state of affairs which provoked it was due to some peculiar degree of wickedness in the nobility and the high officials of the church. Tocqueville, a repentant aristocrat, whose indictment of the Ancien Régime has formed the basis of most later attacks on it, nevertheless knew better. Selfishness, he said, was a vice as old as the world and no more characteristic of one form of society than another, though it manifested itself in different societies in different ways. Comparing the society of pre-Revolutionary France with that of America at the beginning of the nineteenth century, he noted how strong had been the sense of family and kinship in France, and the ties of personal loyalty. These, he believed, could elicit a degree of individual self-sacrifice rarely found in the new societies. On the other hand, he noted how weak in the old societies had been the sense of duty to the community and of obligation to one's neighbour.

The peasants had occasion to know this, notwithstanding the communal organization of agriculture, which was naturally, in a society so organized, used by the strong to oppress the weak. At every level of social life, the people with the greatest wealth and influence framed, twisted or evaded the law to their own advantage. The mass of the peasantry was far from being the only victim of these circumstances, though it suffered most; nor, apart from the state, were the church and the nobility its only oppressors. The record of the bourgeois, who owned many *seigneuries* and farmed the dues in many others, was no better and is often said to have been worse. That of the small class of rich peasants was in some ways worst of all.

The village, like every other group, had its hierarchy. In the more prosperous districts there grew up a class of substantial tenant-farmers, comparable to those in England; but even over the greater part of the country, where the system of share-cropping prevailed, the villages had their *coqs de village*. These were well-to-do peasants, possessing carts and oxen, and enough land to feed their families,

They could sometimes even save enough to buy themselves an office in the neighbouring town, which served their children as a stepping stone for the ascent of the social ladder. In his analysis of the members of the Paris Parlement in the eighteenth century, Professor Bluche tells us that it was not uncommon for peasant families to climb into the nobility in three generations. No class, however, drove harsher bargains than these successful peasants, or showed more skill and effrontery in cheating and intimidating the tax-collectors; and the burdens they evaded, unlike those of the nobility which was separately assessed, fell directly and immediately on their neighbours because of the collective responsibility for the *Taille*.

In the poverty-stricken societies of eighteenth-century Europe, it seemed a law of nature, as Quesnay, the founder of the school of Physiocrats, said, that 'A man can only acquire wealth by means of the wealth he already possesses.'[6] Those who started destitute were more than likely to remain so. Money and education conferred advantages that grew in a geometrical progression, while the poor and ignorant were pushed to the wall. Tocqueville said of the mass of the peasantry that civilization seemed to turn against them alone. They were the predestined victims of a royal policy directed to the pursuit of objects other than agriculture; of a conservatism, of which admittedly they were themselves the principal exponents, that blocked the road to change; and of an administration in which, notwithstanding the paternalistic ideals, educated officials of good-will were too few, and other officials too ignorant, poorly paid and open to bribery and intimidation, to protect the weak against the strong.

It had always been so, and as a result the misery of the peasants had generally been accepted as part of the natural order of things. As one eighteenth-century writer expressed it: 'The habit of suffering they have contracted has killed in them the knowledge that they suffer. It is a kind of ignorance of their misery, and if they know that they are unhappy they know it more or less as we know that we must die. Here is an admirable arrangement of nature; if she causes men to be born in misery she gives them the disposition that makes them able to endure it and even to forget it.'[7]

20 Caricature
of a bourgeoise
aping the
society woman

From the middle of the eighteenth century onwards, however,
two developments occurred to undermine this complacency. One
was the great growth in population which, though it took place in
every European country, had more disturbing consequences in
France than elsewhere because France was more densely populated
to start with. Lefebvre estimated that the numbers of the French
peasantry increased by 2 million between 1770 and 1790. They may
well have increased to a comparable extent in the two previous
decades. The hitherto familiar demographic pattern was disrupted
and the population ceased to be periodically decimated by famine
and epidemics. Among the poorer classes of peasants, who had
always been the principal sufferers from these disasters, many,
as Professor Labrousse put it, thus had their death sentences remitted,
but only in exchange for unemployment or starvation wages. 'The
numbers of our children', the authors of one of the *cahiers* complained
in 1789, 'reduces us to desperation.'[8]

The much higher proportion than in previous ages that lived to grow up caused the continual subdivision of peasant properties – lands, Turgot said, which had barely sufficed for a single family were divided among five or six heirs, each of whom would then divide his portion among five or six others. Many peasants had no land at all. By the time of the Revolution there had grown up a landless proletariat which, in a number of provinces, formed the most numerous class among the peasantry, and whose members found work, when they were fortunate enough to do so, as day-labourers and domestic servants. Often, however, they were not so fortunate, and in these circumstances it became less easy than in the past to take peasant misery for granted, since it increasingly manifested itself in hordes of beggars and vagabonds who threatened the security of the countryside.

It also became less easy for another reason. Hitherto it had always been supposed that man could improve the processes of trade and industry by rational effort, but that the processes of agriculture were largely beyond his control. By the middle of the eighteenth century, the English example had shown that this was not so, and it may well have been the principal reason for the revolution in thinking on economic matters that became widespread in France in the third decade of the eighteenth century. To the school of the Physiocrats, whose ideas influenced the minds of most of France's principal ministers from the 1760s onwards, it was agriculture, not trade, that provided an economy with its dynamic. 'Poor peasants', Quesnay wrote in huge capital letters at the end of one of his 'maxims', 'mean a poor kingdom',[9] and so it came to be widely believed in educated circles in France. It also came to be believed by the rulers in all the other major countries of Europe, as well as in many minor ones.

The concern for the peasant that developed in the second half of the eighteenth century was a product both of humanitarianism and of a sense of the expedient. The latter, however, seems to have been the more powerful. Though Frederick the Great pronounced serfdom to be a disgrace to humanity, and Catherine the Great started her reign with similar views, Frederick, for all his attempts to improve

21 François Quesnay (1694–1774), founder of the school of Physiocrats and of the science of economics. Though the son of a peasant he became the principal physician to Louis XV and Mme de Pompadour and acquired a title of hereditary nobility

Prussian agriculture, did not lighten the burdens on the serfs significantly and Catherine did much to increase them. Both could afford to disregard the peasants because neither was brought into competition with governments that had made any progress towards solving the peasant problem, and also because both were militarily successful. Among the major powers, it was only in France and the Habsburg dominions, whose international position was precarious or declining, that the problem was taken seriously. Maria Theresa was continually preoccupied by it, and with Joseph II it became an obsession. In France the Physiocrats continually rammed home the point that France's status as a great power depended on an answer being found to it.

However misguided some of the Physiocrats' ideas may have been, they observed many facts correctly. They did not need Arthur Young's calculations to show them that much more capital was sunk in the land in England than in France, and that the cross-fertilization of town and country that occurred in England – as a result of which foreign trade increased the wealth of the towns and stimulated the demand for agricultural products, and improvements in agriculture stimulated the demand for manufactured goods – did not occur to any comparable extent in France. Though the French towns grew richer through the growth of trade and manufactures, the wealth that was thus generated was used only to a very small extent to finance agricultural improvement. The poverty of the peasants was in consequence perpetuated, and indeed, because of the growing numbers, increased. Among other causes it set narrower limits to the development of trade and manufactures than existed in England.

## THE PRIVILEGED SOCIETY

### The nature of privilege

Privilege is today a pejorative term used to describe advantages which a person is held to enjoy for reasons other than his own legitimate efforts. It was the Enlightenment which first gave it this meaning. Before then, and indeed in many contexts up to the Revolution, it was a purely legal term, devoid of emotional content, applied to certain kinds of rights enforceable at law. According to a contemporary definition, it meant 'distinctions, whether useful or honorific, which are enjoyed by certain numbers of society and denied to others'.[10] In French official documents a common phrase was 'les nobles et privilégiés', by which was understood simply the nobles and other privileged persons who were exempt from the *Taille* and the taxes and other obligations associated with it.

Privilege in this, to twentieth-century ears, unusual sense could be the property of an individual in his own right, as when the king bestowed on a favourite for his lifetime some concession, such as the proceeds of a particular tax or exemption from particular customs duties. Normally, however, it belonged to people only in their capacity as members of particular groups. Before the days of the

46

22 Aristocratic pleasures: the engraving shows the Yew Tree Ball, a masked ball held in the Hall of Mirrors at Versailles in 1745 to celebrate the ▶ engagement of the Dauphin and Maria Theresa

Enlightenment, opinion on the Continent did not concern itself with the rights of the individual. The British had fought their civil war and made their revolution in 1688 largely on behalf of individual rights; on the Continent, by contrast, it was the rights, or, as it was said, privileges of groups that commanded respect and that were the cause of dispute between the monarchs and their subjects. The difference between the British and the Continental attitude on this matter, before the ideas of the Enlightenment gained general currency, is well illustrated by a conversation which took place, in the autumn of 1749, between Montesquieu, already famous for his *De l'Esprit des Lois*, and Charles Yorke, the son of the British Lord Chancellor, Hardwicke. Charles Yorke explained to Montesquieu how his father had remodelled Scottish law after the Jacobite Rebellion of 1745 and had removed from the chiefs of the Scottish clans their powers of justice. This seemed to him a great achievement but it did not seem so to Montesquieu, who, whatever enlightened notions he might hold in some respects, in this respect defended the old order against the new ideas. Montesquieu said to Yorke that the rights of the Scottish chiefs were 'a barrier against the Crown to prevent the monarchy from running into despotism'; to which Yorke replied that in England 'all private rights, which encroached on the legal authority of the Crown, tended to erect petty tyrants at the expense of the people's liberty'.[11] Montesquieu, however, evidently remained unconvinced.

Rights of this sort were much more extensive in the serf-owning countries of central and eastern Europe than in France. In Russia (in law) and in Prussia and the hereditary lands of the House of Habsburg (in practice), the lord of the manor possessed powers of administration and justice so extensive that they amounted to a virtually complete control over the lives and possessions of his peasants. In the Hohenzollern and Habsburg dominions, indeed, the peasants were officially described as the lord's 'subjects'. The description was exact, since the serf was bound to the soil of the manor, and if he escaped he was guilty of a criminal offence which placed him in the position of an outlaw. Within the manor he was subject, more or less completely, to the landlord's justice. If he committed an

23 Charles-Louis Secondat de Montesquieu, Baron de la Brède (1689–1755). Descended from a noble family of soldiers and magistrates, he inherited in 1716 from an uncle an office in the Parlement of Bordeaux but sold it in 1726 to raise money. Montesquieu was famous throughout Europe for his writings, particularly *De l'Esprit des Lois*

offence against someone from another manor the landlord was held responsible. Though the state imposed taxes on him, it required the landlord to collect them and to make good any deficit.

These arrangements were inescapable because in this part of Europe the populations were too poor, and the number of educated people too small, to permit the creation of a bureaucracy capable of taking over the landlord's functions. In France, where there was more wealth and education, the arm of the state stretched further and the *seigneur* had been shorn of most, though not all, of his administrative and judicial powers. Nevertheless, the confusion between public and private functions, which was characteristic of administration in central and eastern Europe, and the basis of the privileged society, also persisted in France.

24 The Château de la Brède where Montesquieu was born

25 The Premier Président of the Paris Parlement in 1768,
Etienne-François d'Aligre, member of a noble Robe family

Though France was administered by a body of officials owing their
positions theoretically to the royal choice, the king could not afford,
or did not choose to afford, to pay most of them adequate salaries.
As in England at an earlier period, and as in most other Continental
countries in the eighteenth century, public offices in France were sold.
Apart from the principal offices of state, moreover, and in contradistinction to the practice elsewhere, they were sold in perpetuity.
Notoriously this is true of the offices in the Parlements, the most

51

powerful institutions in the kingdom, which were the highest courts of justice, but which also exercised wide powers of administration, and whose consent was necessary before royal edicts had the force of law. It was also true, however, of many offices in other departments of state, and even of offices in the towns and villages which were held by humble people. In all such cases the office was the property of the purchaser, as long as he remained a member of the organization to which it was attached. Subject to certain limitations which, in the Parlements particularly, were considerable, because of the qualifications required of office-holders, the office was his to sell, bequeath or otherwise dispose of as he saw fit. Though by virtue of it he discharged a public function, it was nevertheless his private property, entitling him to privileges, in his private as well as his public capacity, that were both honorific and useful.

These arrangements, which the Crown's perennial need for money encouraged, but for which it was not alone responsible, were typical of a society in which, as Charles Yorke said, the legal authority of the Crown on the one hand, and the rights of the individual on the other, were limited by the rights of groups.

The privileged groups in France were of many different kinds and cannot be subsumed under a single principle. All, however, may be said to have been expressions of a profound belief in inequality, in autonomy and diversity (in contradistinction to the Enlightenment's ideal of centralized and uniform systems of administration), and in hierarchy and discipline; for all were hierarchically organized societies, in which the members were subjected to rules devised and enforced, to a greater or lesser extent, by the group itself.

The communal organization of agriculture had its counterpart in many other spheres of life. The promotion of education in the universities, of the arts and sciences in the academies, of overseas commerce through the chartered companies, of trade and industry through the guilds and other associations, were all activities in which, until the last decades before the Revolution, a person might in general engage only if he joined the appropriate organization, which then subjected him to its discipline and permitted him to enjoy the privileges which belonged to it by virtue of royal grant or consent.

26 The Château of Chenonceaux, the property up to the Revolution of the family of the General Farmer, Claude Dupin, who acquired it in 1733

Privileged groups also dominated social relations and played an important part in government and administration. Society was divided into orders or estates; the Parlements, though organs of state, were largely self-governing, self-recruiting corporations, whose members were subjected to a particular code of law and possessed, in accordance with their positions in the hierarchy, particular useful and honorific rights. The indirect taxes were collected, most of the royal monopolies managed, and most of the royal loans raised, by the company of General Farmers – a private company subject to a considerable degree of royal control, but, to an even greater extent than the Parlements, self-governing and self-recruiting. This organization was the largest employer of labour in the country, apart from the armed forces. Its leading members were believed to be among the richest men in the community. Its privileges included the authority to maintain a police numbering, by 1784, twenty-three thousand men with 'an almost unlimited and arbitrary right of search over the premises, domiciles and persons of all private subjects at any hour on any day without court warrant'.[12]

Besides the groups whose privileges were in theory, if not in practice, related to their functions, there were the privileged territories – villages, towns, provinces and other geographical areas, whose inhabitants, or the more favoured sections among them, enjoyed special rights by virtue of living in the locality. For example, the so-called *Pays d'États* – provinces most of which had been united to the French Crown after the rise of absolutism and allowed to keep their liberties – regularly got off with a much lighter tax-burden than the other provinces. In the so-called *villes franches*, which included all the major towns in the country, the people with the freedom of the city had virtually emancipated themselves from direct taxation and were exempt from the servile obligations of the *corvée*, and service in the militia.

The privileges which could accrue to the members of all these privileged groups were infinitely various; nevertheless, they fall into the two broad categories used by the writer of the passage quoted earlier. Some were 'honorific', that is, conferred prestige: for example, the right of the nobleman to carry a sword and the right of the *seigneur* to an enclosed pew in the chancel of the church, to be sprinkled with holy water apart from the rest of the congregation, and to have the church draped in black when a death occurred in his family. Others were 'useful', that is, conferred a material advantage: for example, the *seigneur*'s right to payment in money or in kind from those subject to his authority; the right of the nobleman and the bourgeois of the *villes franches* to exemption from the *Taille*; the exclusive right of the members of the trading and professional associations to the discharge of whatever functions it was the purpose of the association to fulfil.

Because privilege could take so many different forms, and because it penetrated into so many spheres of social, political and economic life, everyone, apart from those with no fixed domicile or occupation, can be said to have been privileged in some degree, since all belonged to one or more groups with special rights. When, nevertheless, the subject came up for discussion under the Ancien Régime (and no subject was more commonly discussed), attention was usually focused on the so-called 'privileged orders'.

27 Judge and Consuls of the Bordeaux Bourse

In France – and there were comparable institutions elsewhere – these were the first order, or estate, of the church and the second order, or estate, of the nobility. All the principal posts of power and prestige belonged to members of these estates. The estates themselves, however, were described as privileged, not by virtue of this fact, but because of the useful and honorific rights which membership of them conferred. The widespread assumption that the nobles and clergy were the only privileged people in France and other countries in the eighteenth century is due partly to a confusion over the meaning of words, and partly to the propaganda of the 1780s and afterwards. In Turgot's all-embracing vision the privileges of estates, guilds, provinces and the rest, were all equally sinister impediments to justice, efficiency and the increase of wealth. But the writers of the Enlightenment usually, and the revolutionaries always, gave the word a new meaning, emphasizing some kinds of privilege to the exclusion of others.

In the terminology of the pre-enlightened age, it has been shown, privilege meant the legal rights enjoyed by various categories of people, often on a hereditary basis, by virtue of the royal consent

55

or grant. To the apostles of the Enlightenment it commonly meant any kind of advantage, but particularly wealth, which a person had not earned (or which in the writer's opinion he had not earned) by service to the community. A privileged person thus came to seem a person in fortunate circumstances he had done nothing to deserve. Many members of the privileged orders, admittedly, could be so described and provided the most conspicuous examples of privilege in this sense. The condition of many others, however, was often very miserable, since the nobleman's legal rights did not necessarily confer either wealth or prestige.

To the English-speaking world, the privileged orders have usually seemed mysterious, and particularly the order, or estate, of the nobility to which, even in the Middle Ages, there was no exact equivalent in England. In most of the Continental countries in the eighteenth century, the nobility included not only people who corresponded in social status to the British aristocracy; it also included people who corresponded to the English gentry, and many others who could not have aspired even to this position because they were too poor. These differences arose because, by the eighteenth century, the Continental nobility was a legal category but not a social class, as the term is most commonly understood – that is, a body of people with comparable incomes and a common way of life. In the early Middle Ages, when the nobleman found his principal occupation and pleasure in fighting, differences in rank, wealth and prestige, as Marc Bloch has pointed out, 'did not produce any profound breach in the unity of class consciousness'.[13] Since those primitive and warlike times, however, the growth in the importance of money, and of education and refinement, had widened the gap between rich and poor.

The British aristocracy in the eighteenth century possessed titles recognized in law, but it had hardly any other legal privileges, and the gentry had none at all. A variety of causes combined to ensure that the British aristocrats were both rich and small in numbers; in particular, their political power enabled them to prevent the sale of titles which had been common before the Civil War, and a title descended only to the eldest son. The members of the gentry, which

28 The 'Capitouls' of Toulouse were the municipal magistrates. Their office, purchasable and greatly desired by rich *roturiers*, conferred hereditary nobility

was distinguished from the groups below it only by a combination of birth and money, could not maintain their positions if they lost their wealth. Among the English upper classes, wealth and social status were thus allied, but there was virtually no privilege in the Continental sense of the term.

On the Continent, too, as must be shown presently, it proved impossible to keep wealth and social status apart. The nobles' privileges, however, did not necessarily confer either the one or the other, because they descended from a father to all his children, no matter what financial misfortunes might overtake the family – at least up to the point when its members were forced into *dérogeance*. *Dérogeance* was an offence at law which deprived a man of his noble status. It provided a mechanism, to which there was a counterpart in other groups, by which the unsatisfactory members could be expelled. A man became guilty of it if he committed certain crimes (for example, treason), or if he engaged in various occupations thought unfitting for a gentleman, into which he might be forced by

57

poverty. Admittedly, since the end of the sixteenth century the rigours of the law had continually been modified, sometimes for the benefit of particular groups of nobles or individuals, and sometimes in general, as in the ordinance of 1629 which laid down that ship-owning and participation in overseas commerce did not constitute *dérogeance*. Retail trade, however, continued to remain forbidden; and in any case, whatever the law, public opinion and, no doubt equally significantly, lack of capital prevented most nobles from engaging in commercial and industrial activities. Poverty and noble status were thus frequently allied. Arthur Young, for example, had aristocratic friends in France who, as he pointed out, were as rich as English dukes, but he also came across noblemen who were struggling to bring up families on £26 a year. One might suppose that a family with an annual income of £100,000 or more can have little in common with one that has only £26. Though all nobles were conscious of having common functions, the usual relations between them were not those of a class with common interests, but those of different classes riven by dissensions between rich and poor.

In the Middle Ages the privileged orders, like many other groups, had been more nearly analogous to a modern fighting service than to a social class, since they were seen as bodies of people subject to a particular code of law and fulfilling a particular function by means of a hierarchy of rank. Just as the members of the church existed to serve God, so it was supposed that the members of the nobility existed to serve the king in the army, at court, or in the civil administration. This idea prevailed until the Revolution. Under the Ancien Régime all noblemen looked on service to the Crown as proper, desirable and necessary – proper because it was the end for which they conceived themselves to have been created; desirable because it brought money, power and prestige; necessary because without it poverty was usually inescapable. In the eighteenth century, however, large numbers of nobles were prevented from entering the royal service because they lacked the capital necessary to buy a commission in the army or a civilian office.

Many members of the privileged orders or estates were poorer than many members of the third estate which was not privileged, and this had always been so. The third estate included everyone who was not a noble or a cleric. Peasants, urban workers, professional people, merchants and other members of the business community all belonged to it. So diverse a body plainly could not be subject to common rules and endowed with special rights, as were the first two estates. Yet most of its members, as has been shown, belonged to privileged groups by virtue of their occupations or the places in which they lived; and although, as *roturiers*, their honorific privileges were always smaller than those of the nobility, whose functions as servants of God and the king were held to be more distinguished, their useful privileges were often larger. The useful privileges of the noble landowner were exercised at the expense of a poverty-stricken agriculture and in general yielded small returns; those of many bourgeois gave them rights in relation to trade, industry and finance, which were much more lucrative. No complaint was more common or more bitter than that the noble landowner who lived from agriculture was doubly subject to direct taxation – because his tenants paid the *Taille* and had correspondingly less to give him in rent, and because after 1749 his own income was also regularly taxed – while the owners of wealth acquired in trade, industry and finance got off scot-free.

The most famous of the attacks on privilege was launched by Sieyès in his *Qu'est-ce que le Tiers État*, first published in 1789. Many writers have taken it as a statement of fact instead of for what it was: a piece of propaganda and a call to battle. Sieyès attempted to make out – though his argument could not take in anyone who follows it closely – that the members of the privileged orders were the only privileged people in France. He compared them to 'those vegetable tumours which live only from the sap of the plants they . . . suck dry'.

The comparison was, however, inexact. If privilege is understood in the old sense of legal rights, then the nobility constituted only one among many privileged groups, and had useful privileges that were less extensive than those of many bourgeois. If it is understood in the new sense of wealth unearned by service to the community, then many, if not most, nobles were excluded by their poverty from the category of the privileged. By suggesting that only the members of the privileged orders had privileges, and that all were privileged in both senses of the term, Sieyès misled his contemporaries as well as later generations. He claimed that privilege was the prerogative of only a small number of people, whose elimination would restore society to health. This, however, was not true. Privilege could not, as Sieyès maintained, be appropriately compared to a tumour, which a simple operation can remove, but was more nearly comparable to a cancer. In its original sense of legal rights, many of which exempted their owners from what later came to be held as the common obligations of citizenship, privilege was an integral part of the social order. Since time immemorial it had seemed the prerequisite of all social activity, as equality before the law was to seem in the nineteenth century. Its natural tendency to proliferate increasingly made the tasks of government impossible.

By the middle of the eighteenth century, privilege had assumed grotesque proportions in France and was beginning to do so in many other countries. The monarchs, and particularly the absolute monarchs who had larger opportunities than their predecessors, had

29 Caricature of
the Abbé Sieyès

always sold privileges for money or granted them in return for services for which they could not afford to pay. In France, where the wealth of the trading community on the one hand, and the costs of war and government on the other, were larger than in most other Continental countries, the opportunities both to buy and to sell privilege were particularly tempting. Louis XIV financed his wars to a large extent by the sale of offices, many of which carried with them patents of nobility and the attendant rights, and all of which conferred some degree of immunity from national obligations. As his successors followed his practice, privilege bred privilege, for any useful privilege, by definition, exempted its possessors from obligations which consequently fell the more heavily on those who lacked it; and the latter, as a result, seized whatever means were available to them to ease their burdens. They resorted to protests or threats, or to bribery if they had the means. Moved sometimes by pity, but more commonly by fear or the need for ready money, the kings or their officials then appeased the more conspicuous among their victims by granting them privileges in their turn.

30 In the eighteenth century Bordeaux was, after London, the largest port in Europe. Its prosperity was built up principally on the trades in sugar from the West Indies.

By the middle of the eighteenth century in France, and at the same time or later in the other Continental monarchies, these practices came to threaten every administration with chaos, which was indeed a word commonly used by officials in many countries to describe the conditions in which they had to operate. It was impossible to conduct administration in an orderly way so long as the law, to use Calonne's words, contained such a 'prodigious multitude'[14] of special provisions. Reforms were exceptionally difficult to introduce, because the confusion in the law deprived administrators of a basis on which to act. Turgot, for example, when he was *Intendant* of Limoges, continually complained of the months of grinding work he had put in merely in order to discover the sums which the various individuals subject to his authority were supposed to pay in taxes. There was the further difficulty that all the special provisions involved rights of property, whose removal seemed calculated to cause their owners loss of material benefits or prestige; and the defence of property, it increasingly came to be emphasized, was the principal function of the state. Not surprisingly, in these circumstances, a large number of administrators and writers in France in the second half of the eighteenth century, and a growing number in other countries, began to look for salvation to the *droit commun* which Sieyès was later to invoke – that is, to the creation of a body of rights, to which all citizens were entitled, and of obligations, from which none were exempt.

## The beneficiaries

Though all nobles were privileged in the sense of enjoying the special rights which belonged to the members of the nobility as such, many, it was said earlier, were not privileged in the sense of enjoying a favoured position in society. The revolutionary leader, Brissot (himself the thirteenth son of a pastry-cook in Chartres), said in 1790, 'If there is any order of citizens who are the victims of despotism and the aristocracy of the rich and the great it is the poor nobility, that numerous class of gentlemen farmers, confined by a gothic prejudice to a single estate.'[15]

The men, women and children of noble birth in France in 1789 are generally supposed to have numbered about 400,000; and at present we lack the data to estimate how many of them were poor enough to have deserved Brissot's description. The author of the principal work on the French nobility in the eighteenth century, H. Carré, writing in 1920, said that one could 'multiply indefinitely the examples of needy gentlefolk reduced to misery'.[16] It used to be accepted that the nobles in this condition formed the majority, and there is as yet no valid evidence to the contrary, despite the increasing number of the well-to-do that modern research is bringing to light, for between the very rich and the very poor there were many gradations. In the neighbourhood of the major provincial towns, there seems usually to have been a prosperous group of nobles, such as Robert Forster has described in his *Nobility of Toulouse in the Eighteenth Century*. The twenty richest noblemen of this district, who formed the subject of his study, lived in varying degrees of comfort and even elegance. They owned estates that consisted, on an average, of from 200 to 300 acres. They held the principal offices in Toulouse and in the provincial Parlement. The more successful bourgeois bought offices and entered their ranks. As the largest landowners in the neighbourhood, and the holders of the most important judicial and administrative offices, they dominated local society.

Similar or more prosperous groups existed in the vicinity of Bordeaux and the other major ports. Lefebvre, in his study of the Orléanais, discovered their equivalents there. Plainly, nobles of their type were to be found in many parts of France, and were the privileged people in the provinces in the modern sense of the word 'privilege'.

By eighteenth-century standards, however, their privileges were not large. Many were too poor to afford a carriage and, if they spent the winter in the neighbouring town, could aspire to nothing better than lodgings. Even those who maintained considerable establishments could not afford to stay in Paris for any length of time or, often, even to visit it. Their average incomes, in the cases where they have been calculated, were much lower than those of the members of English county society. If the families Robert Forster studied are typical, and Arthur Young's judgements support his description, they were frugal, austere and thrifty. As Arthur Young said: 'Where one gentleman of small property in the provinces of France runs out his fortune, there are ten such in England that do it.'[17] Though conservative and averse from innovations, like the smaller nobility in other countries at the time, they devoted much attention to the running of their estates, as indeed they felt obliged to do in order to make ends meet.

The privileged *par excellence* under the Ancien Régime were not these people, fortunate though they may have been by comparison with the bulk of the population, but the few hundred families who constituted Paris society, and who formed what Henry James was later to describe as the world of power and pleasure. In many cases their incomes were as large as those of the aristocrats in England, notwithstanding the much greater poverty of France. They were the people whom, for centuries, the French had been accustomed to call *Les Grands* and for whose particular benefit, it began to appear increasingly in the second half of the eighteenth century, government and society were organized. In Talleyrand's famous phrase (and Ségur spoke of them in similar terms), they enjoyed a 'douceur de vivre' that no future generations were to know in France.

31 The château of a provincial nobleman in easy circumstances—Pinsaguel, near Toulouse, the property of the Marquis de Bertier, whose family had owned it since 1495. The Bertiers had risen through trade and the purchase of municipal office which conferred hereditary nobility

32 The Duc de Choiseul married into the family of the rich financier, Crozat. This miniature from his *tabatière* shows the *premier salon* and the dressing-room in his Paris house, the Hôtel Crozat de Châtel

Since human happiness and misery are states of mind it is impossible to measure them. The idyllic picture of life as lived by *Les Grands* under the Ancien Régime may, nevertheless, be exaggerated. Horace Walpole, who spent several months in Paris in 1765, observed with irritation that his aristocratic acquaintances, unlike their counterparts in London, were continually preoccupied with problems of philosophy and politics, and with what they described as the 'abuses' of the régime, so that, as he said, 'they may be growing wise but the intermediate passage is dullness'.[18] A recent student of French attitudes to happiness in the eighteenth century, Robert Mauzi, has seen in the interminable discussions on this subject that went on in the *salons* the proof of a profound malaise and awareness of unhappiness. Thoughtful people at that time, he concluded, found it impossible to be happy in the midst of misery and in a society from which order and progress seemed absent. Though

Talleyrand spoke of 'la douceur de vivre', Malesherbes spoke of 'le mal de vivre'. The Ancien Régime may well have appeared a golden age only to the victims of the Revolution in retrospect, and to the young men like Ségur, who believed himself to be on the threshold of a new era in which liberal principles would prevail, but who was also the heir to wealth and a famous name which he did not suppose to be in jeopardy.

Materially speaking, nevertheless, the privileges of *Les Grands* were very large in both the old and the new senses of the word. By definition, these people occupied all the principal posts of power and prestige and were the richest group in the country. Though it was easy to run through a fortune in this milieu, and though to enter it one needed wealth in the first instance, the possessors of great fortunes naturally gravitated towards it, and the greatest fortunes could not be made or retained without political influence. By definition, too, all *Les Grands* were nobles, since the material and social advantages of a title, on the one hand, and the ease with which it could be acquired, on the other, had always been so great, that it would have been unthinkable at any time that they should be *roturiers*.

The legend that Louis XIV favoured the bourgeoisie at the expense of the nobility has as much and as little substance as the similar legend about the Tudors. Himself the greatest aristocrat in Europe, Louis had no interest in the trading community except as a source of money for his wars and his court. As he said, however, he did not intend to share his power with the great noble families, and in any case the expansion in State activity that occurred in his reign demanded men of administrative ability that these families could hardly have provided. Louis thus promoted people of inferior birth to high office. But he gave them titles to correspond with their new positions, as well as great opportunities to acquire wealth for themselves and their relations; thus he preserved the principle of aristocracy while changing its personnel.

The kind of ruling class we associate with France in the eighteenth century, and with other European countries at the same time or later, was born of this marriage (which Professor Hans Rosenberg

33, 34 From Robe to Sword. Left, the Marquis de Maillebois (1682–1762), the most distinguished military commander of the Ancien Régime after Marshal Saxe. He was the son of Nicolas Desmarets, nephew of Colbert and Contrôleur Général from 1708–15. Right, the Duc de Belleisle (1684–1761), field-marshal and negotiator of the confederacy against Maria Theresa in 1741, commander of the French and Bavarian armies that invaded Austria in that year. He was the grandson of Nicolas Fouquet (*see Ill. 94*)

has shown to be as characteristic of Prussia as of France) between the great families and the *parvenus* who had acquired titles through wealth or service in the formative period of absolutism. During the half-century after Louis XIV's death the social gulf, which in his reign had separated the courtiers and, to a large extent, the army officers, from the holders of the more important civilian posts, was to all intents and purposes obliterated. The distinction between the army and the Robe (that is, the members of the Parlements and other sovereign courts of justice, from which the ministers and other high officials were usually recruited) became, at the top of each profession, one of function only. Though families tended to retain their tradition of service in the one or the other capacity, they nevertheless intermarried continually. Many Robe families had sons in the army, and many army families sons in the Robe. Men even changed from one profession to the other. Though it continued to be fashionable to laugh at the nobles of the Robe for their stiff and formal

behaviour – the Duc de Lévis once observed that Calonne was the only one of them who behaved like a gentleman – these strictures need not be taken literally. They were an expression of the pleasure which people found in contemplating the finer shades of social distinctions and which Tocqueville saw as characteristic of aristo-

35, 36 The pleasures of *Les Grands*: left, *Renaud dans les Jardins d'Armide*, a scene from Quinault's opera, performed in Paris in 1761 and 1764. Above, a performance of an *opéra comique* in the Salle de la Comédie Italienne

cratic societies. As Professor Bluche has shown, among the magistrates of the Paris Parlement between 1717 and 1771, the proportion who were of 'ancienne race' (that is, could trace their nobility back to 1400 or 1500) was as high as the proportion in the nobility as a whole.

As a result of these developments, the ascent to power became at a certain stage more difficult. It was no longer possible in the second half of the eighteenth century to rise from such humble beginnings as Colbert's to such high office as he came to hold. With the passage of time the tasks of government became more complicated and routines more firmly established. The monarchs everywhere came to realize that they could not disrupt the social and professional hierarchies as they had done when absolutism was a new and revolutionary force. Even that innovator and tyrant, Frederick William I of Prussia, was driven to admit at the end of his life that, as he put it in his inimitable German, he must 'soutenieren', or give support to, the body of his servants, if he wished himself to be 'souteniert'; and this, as his more famous son recognized, meant allowing the established nobility to occupy most of the important posts, and granting titles to bourgeois only in small numbers and as a reward for outstanding service.

In France, as a result of trends that were similar though not so strong, the nobles of the Robe acquired, as they did in other countries, a greater degree of power; and this they used, among other ways, to exclude outsiders, and to insist on promotion in accordance with procedures established by themselves. No manifestations of this tendency are more notorious than the provisions of the French Parlements in the 1770s that confined the higher posts in their corporations to people who could show four generations of nobility on the father's side, and the similar provision which was introduced into many regiments in the army by the law of 1781.

Given the state of public opinion when they were introduced, these measures could hardly have been more unfortunate. Their practical effects, however, have often been misinterpreted. They have commonly been adduced in proof of the fact that, as Tocqueville said, the nobility was becoming more and more of a caste and closing its ranks against the bourgeoisie, to an extent that kings in the past would not have tolerated. These statements are exaggerations and in some respects even untrue. In the first place, the people principally outraged by the provisions requiring aspirants to certain offices to prove that their families had been noble for four generations were

37 Antoine-Pierre-Joseph-Marie Barnave (1761–93), a prominent member of the Constituent Assembly and one of the most profound critics of the Ancien Régime. Here he is shown addressing a meeting of the three estates at the château of Vizille, near Grenoble, during the revolt in the Dauphiné of 1788

not the *roturiers* but those who had had titles for three generations or less. In the second place, the provisions could not be enforced. Anyone with enough money could prove that he had the appropriate ancestors, for the forging of genealogies had been a flourishing industry since Louis XIV's reign. In any case, some Parlements seem to have been prepared, like the Parlement of Grenoble in Barnave's case, to waive their regulations when the candidate was otherwise suitable. Finally, though the avenues leading to the heights of prestige and power were, in the last stages of the ascent, harder to climb at the end of the eighteenth century than earlier, entrance to them, in the opinion of contemporaries and even of Tocqueville, was easier than in the past. Though Tocqueville said, in one place in his *Ancien Régime*, that the nobility was becoming more and more of a caste, in another place he said that a title had never been so easy to get.

By selling titles on a huge scale to finance his wars, as well as offices carrying patents of nobility, which people were often virtually forced to buy, Louis XIV had ensured that all bourgeois of substance entered the nobility. They had, indeed, means of doing this even without his help by the purchase of *seigneuries* which, in the course of time, in fact though not in law, conferred a prescriptive right to noble status. The same or comparable practices continued throughout the eighteenth century. Though the more desirable offices became harder to get, the total number of offices, according to the calculations of Professor Martin Göhring, increased by a percentage not much smaller than the percentage increase in the general population. Voltaire once said that anyone who wanted to could become a marquis. Anyone with enough money could acquire, as Voltaire did himself, the office of King's Secretary: a pure sinecure, costing the equivalent of £5000 in the English currency of the time and carrying with it hereditary nobility and its attendant privileges.

The law of 1781 relating to the army and other similar provisions were not in fact designed to keep aspiring bourgeois out of the nobility. On the contrary, the government continued to facilitate their entry. The purpose of the provisions was to safeguard the claims of the older and poorer noble families against those of the richer and more recently ennobled, particularly those who had made their money in finance. These provisions represented a reaction against the policies of previous kings, and especially of Louis XIV. Louis XIV, however, had created bourgeois *gentilshommes* on an unprecedented scale. What the restrictive measures of the 1770s and 1780s attempted to achieve was little more than the ordinary workings of the social system had achieved in England after 1660. In England, even in the nineteenth century, it was said that it took three generations to make a gentleman, and high civilian and military office remained the gentleman's prerogative. In France, the demand was for four generations, but it was impossible to enforce. Money earned in commerce, and particularly in finance, seems to have exercised a more immediate influence on social and official status than it did either in the poorer aristocracies of the other European monarchies, where there were fewer wealthy bourgeois, or in the richer aristocracy of England, where estates were in general larger and more prosperous, and where the need to marry into the business world was proportionately smaller. In what English county in the same period would it be possible to find a parallel to the situation which Professor Goubert has described in the Beauvaisis, where, of fifty-eight noblemen who assembled to draw up their list of grievances in 1789, only ten could trace their origins back to the beginning of the seventeenth century, most dated from the reign of Louis XIV, and sixteen from the period after 1740?

Yet in spite of the part played by money in French society, it was seen there, as in the other European aristocracies, as a means to an end and not as an end in itself. Entry into the circle of the great, in France as elsewhere, was achieved by means of a combination of attributes – birth, high office, intelligence, skill in the ways of the world, as well as wealth. A deficiency in any one of these could be compensated for by a higher degree of the others. In general, wealth was nevertheless essential, and particularly so in Paris, because *Les Grands* could not have maintained their prestige if the expenditure of any other group had been greater than theirs. In the groups where money was made on a large scale, however, the highest prestige equally seemed impossible without a title and its attendant privileges which, in the course of time, enabled a family to consider itself of noble blood. Duclos expressed the current prejudices when he said, 'the pride of wealth is different from the pride of birth. The one has something unconstrained about it which seems to elicit a legitimate admiration. The other has a revolting vulgarity which savours of usurpation.'[19] From the desire of the rich bourgeois to escape the stigma of vulgarity and of the poor nobleman to escape the constraints of poverty, there emerged that state of affairs described by Duclos: 'There are few fortunes that do not find their way into the distinguished families . . . without the commerce which has grown up between pride and necessity most of the noble houses would fall into misery and in consequence into obscurity.'[20]

Money thus came to be the great leveller. It was seen as a rising tide which burst through the dikes that had isolated the privileged orders from the rest of the population. 'By its very nature', Sénac de Meilhan said, 'wealth tends to reduce those who possess it to the same level. Neither rank nor privilege can resist its sovereign power . . . it divides society into classes in accordance with their degrees of opulence.'[21] In France, wealth did so indeed, and in the process destroyed the basis in reality that the order or estate of the nobility had possessed in the past.

In provincial society in Toulouse, Robert Forster tells us, noblemen moved in each other's company on a footing of equality and, with some exception for the dukes and princes of the blood, it was commonly said that *Les Grands* did the same. Even the tax-farmers, all of whom had titles, came to be received in the *salons*. How different, Sénac de Meilhan lamented, from the days of Louis XIV, when the great Condé, in a magnanimous mood, had once challenged to a duel a nobleman of inferior rank whom he had insulted, and this man, overcome by so much condescension (for duels were fought only between equals), had 'immediately thrown his sword at the Prince's feet and embraced his knees'.[22] Turgot wrote in 1776: 'The cause of privilege is no longer the cause of the distinguished families against the *roturiers*, but the cause of the rich against the poor.'[23]

This state of affairs is a testimony to the accuracy of Tocqueville's insight when he said (though the facts he cited in support of his point were often wrong) that before the Revolution the new society already existed in the womb of the old. The French aristocracy of the Ancien Régime was a new phenomenon. The very word itself was new. We speak of the nobles of the Middle Ages but of the aristocrats of the eighteenth century, and by the aristocrats we commonly mean *Les Grands* – the ruling class – whose counterparts endured in the other Continental monarchies throughout the nineteenth century, in a form modelled partly on the French and partly on the English, whom the French themselves in the eighteenth century aspired to imitate in many ways.

The eighteenth-century aristocracy is not to be identified with the nobles in general, most of whom were too poor to associate with it; nor – though this accusation was often brought against it during the Revolution – were its standards solely derived from the feudal past. *Les Grands*, it was the fashion to say at the time, had shed many of

38 Charles Pinot Duclos (1704–72), author of *Considérations sur les Moeurs* and other works. The son of a hat-maker ennobled by the king, he became historiographer royal in 1750, in succession to Voltaire, and was Secretary of the Académie Française from 1754

their forefathers' characteristics and adopted many others that distinguished the rich bourgeois of their day. In proof of this were adduced not only the importance *Les Grands* attached to money and the growing spirit of equality which prevailed among them, but their smaller addiction to pomp, display and formality, and their greater addiction to comfort, elegance, refinement and cultivation. Tocqueville noted, and recent researches have confirmed him, that the differences in styles of living between the richest members of the bourgeoisie and the leading nobles, both in the provinces and in Paris, had diminished to the point where the more socially gifted and intelligent in the first group could accommodate themselves without much difficulty to the manners of the second. The success with which this transformation could be effected received its supreme illustrations from the career of Voltaire and, after his death, that of Benjamin Franklin, a man of humble origins but great ability and charm, who inherited Voltaire's position as the idol of the *salons*.

75

39 Fashionable tea-party 'English style' in the Princesse de Conti's *salon*: the young Mozart is at the piano, Président Hénault of the Paris Parlement is seated (right ▶ background) in front of the folding screen

The extent, however, to which the aristocrats accepted standards that may be described as bourgeois, was limited and often superficial. In many significant ways they remained bound by their past. Whatever attitudes they may have retained from the bourgeois world from which they sprang, or learned from the recently ennobled with whom they consorted, many ideals dating back to the early Middle Ages commanded a deeper allegiance. Only too obviously many aristocrats had owed their positions in the fairly recent past not to birth but to royal grant, commonly bestowed in return for money. It is generally accepted that not more than about 6 per cent of the French nobility in 1789 were of 'ancienne race' and that very few had been noble for as much as six generations. Nevertheless, it was on their blood that they prided themselves. When in the 1780s and afterwards they were described as a 'caste', this was not because they constituted a caste in fact, but because a caste was what they would have liked above all to constitute. Their attitude was succinctly expressed, as late as 1839, by two aristocratic travellers who met on a ship bound for St Petersburg. One was a Frenchman, the Marquis de Custine, and the other his Russian acquaintance, whom he described as Prince K——. They fell to discussing their ancestors and concluded that 'a sovereign can create princes; education, circumstances, genius . . . can create heroes; none of all this can produce a gentleman. . . . La noblesse . . . tient au sang'[24] – nobility is a matter of blood.

The nobleman's blood, it was supposed, bred in him certain characteristics, which were fortified by education in a noble household, which set him apart from other men, and which were expressed in his sense of honour.

The eighteenth-century aristocrat's conception of honour received its classic formulation in Montesquieu's *De l'Esprit des Lois*, which became the nobleman's bible all over Europe, was quoted by Hungarian gentry who ordinarily never opened a book, and provided the Russian aristocracy with its inspiration.

Honour, Montesquieu said, is 'the child and father of the nobility' and 'the universal master that must be our constant guide'. It requires that virtue should have 'a certain nobility, behaviour a certain frankness, manners a certain politeness'. It praises actions, not 'because they are good but because they are beautiful, not because they are just but because they are grand, not because they are reasonable but because they are exceptional'. 'It is born of the desire to distinguish oneself.' 'It permits chicanery when this is combined with grandeur of spirit or of action, as in politics.' It requires that one should be 'bold and free' and indifferent to public opinion. 'Above all things it requires of the nobility that they should serve the king in war.' It has its 'supreme rules', of which 'the principal ones are that it is permitted us to take account of our fortune but it is supremely forbidden us to take account of our life'.[25]

These words provided the aristocrat with his standards. Though honour was understood somewhat differently by the aristocracies of different countries – particularly in Prussia it seems to have acquired a peculiar connotation – there were nevertheless everywhere certain ways of behaving which it forbade and others which it prescribed. Above all, in France, it contained an anarchic element, because it made submission to discipline seem servile. Everywhere it exalted service to the king and (particularly in the Roman Catholic countries) to God, above all other professions. Though it did not require, as Montesquieu said, that a man should be indifferent to money, it always seemed incompatible with the productive occupations that increased the wealth of communities.

The merits and defects of honour as an ideal were most strikingly illustrated in North America before the British conquest of Canada. There the British colonists were farmers, traders and seafarers who lived in separate, self-governing communities without a central government or standing army. The Canadians, who owed their existence to the state-sponsored schemes of Colbert, and whose society and government had been modelled on those of metropolitan France, were organized for war. The British colonists prospered and multiplied, while Canada increasingly became an economic liability to the French government. For all this, however, it was the French, not the British, who had the great exploits of daring to their credit. Inspired principally by a love of risk and danger, and by romantic visions of a great empire to lay at the feet of the King of France, it

was they who discovered the Great Lakes and the Rockies, found the source of the Mississippi and went down it to the Gulf of Mexico.

In Europe, similarly, the cult of honour was at variance with the economic needs of the time. Many nobles, as stated earlier, were thrifty and prudent in the management of their estates. As in England, and for that matter also in Russia and the hereditary lands of the House of Habsburg, those possessing estates with mineral resources developed them, and in mining and metallurgy nobles predominated. In spite of this, as Arthur Young continually pointed out, nobles were in general conservative, particularly in matters of agriculture. Like their counterparts in other countries in the eighteenth and nineteenth centuries, though they admitted into their ranks the people who had made money in commerce and industry, in the fusion of values that resulted it was their values on the whole that predominated. The ideal of the ambitious bourgeois was always to 'live nobly', that is, to abandon his money-making activities as soon as he could for the life of a gentleman.

40 Aristocratic idyll: detail of the *Fête à St-Cloud*, by Fragonard, *c.* 1775

Under the Ancien Régime in France, as in other countries, the Court, which was the principal centre of extravagant consumption, encouraged these tendencies and at the same time provided the means of satisfying them. The accusation commonly brought against *Les Grands*, and against their counterparts in other countries at a later date, was that, of the money that was sucked out of the countryside by direct and indirect taxation, and passed into the hands of the government, a large part ultimately found its way into their pockets; for it was a principle among the absolute monarchs to build up the fortunes of their favourites and servants, and to sustain those of the great families, by means of gifts, pensions, monopolies and other perquisites. While the French monarchs created offices and sinecures which they sold for money, they helped *Les Grands* to accumulate the money with which the offices were bought. It is said that there were more generals in the French army than in all the other European armies put together; there were, indeed, so many that they had to exercise their functions in rotation.

81

Equally, much of the money raised in France by taxation that passed into the hands of the tax-farmers and other financial officials, and of the money earned in commerce and industry which, for the reasons already explained, could not be taxed, also found its way into the pockets of *Les Grands* as a result of marriage, and because the tax-farmers and other rich men bought titles and entered high society.

By these means *Les Grands* became the principal beneficiaries, not only of the tribute levied from agriculture, but also of the expanding sector of the economy whose operations they largely dictated. The expanding industries were the luxury industries, and the expanding colonial trades were trades in luxury commodities; so that even eighteenth-century writers who were hostile to the régime often had an ambivalent attitude to luxury because, however reprehensible it might seem in the midst of so much misery, it was nevertheless a major source of employment.

It was also the growing wealth of the towns which made possible the refinement and the culture which *Les Grands* enjoyed *par excellence*, and by virtue of which they saw themselves, not without justice, as the standard-bearers of civilization; for whatever indictments can be brought against them, no ruling class has ever shown greater respect for artistic and intellectual achievement and for the arts of living.

*Les Grands* thus formed the hub of a universe that revolved round them. The worlds of the Court, of the army, of arts and letters, of commerce, industry and finance, functioned principally for their benefit and in response to their needs; and it was for this reason that the Physiocrats, in a formulation that seemed strange to later generations though it was natural in the circumstances, saw all these as 'sterile' – commerce and industry included. Quesnay said, wrongly but plausibly, that the source of all wealth was the land, and he saw the land as being progressively impoverished because of the contributions it was forced to make to the privileged who could pull the strings of power.

The conditions which existed in France in the second half of the eighteenth century were repeated, to a greater or lesser extent,

41, 42, 43 The style of living of *Les Grands*.
A *salon* in the Hôtel Soubise in the Rue des
Francs Bourgeois, Paris, one of the finest
examples of Rococo interior decoration.
Below left, commode by Charles Cressent;
right, sécrétaire by François Oeben

whenever the absolute monarchies and their aristocracies were exposed to the temptations provided by a rapidly developing commerce and the competition in extravagant living to which it gave rise. Many of the same complaints began to be heard in Prussia at the turn of the eighteenth century that had become vocal in France fifty years or more earlier. An impoverished Prussian count, whose poverty excluded him from the circle of the great, wrote in 1795 that a title benefits a man only if he has money, 'that power which dominates everything'. The best jobs are only to be had by influence, which is impossible without money. Advancement goes to the rich. Mere 'merit determines little or nothing'.[26]

Complaints of this sort in Prussia fell on deaf ears until after the débâcle of Jena in 1806. In France, however, in the second half of the eighteenth century, many of *Les Grands*, living as they did in a country whose military power was declining and whose economic foundations were being eroded by the growth of peasant poverty, could not fail to reproach themselves, as aristocrats in other countries were to do later, with the luxury which they enjoyed and which their ideology could be made to condone but not to justify.

44 Invitation cards to the entertainments arranged by Mme de Pompadour for Louis XV in her *petits appartements* were much coveted and a great honour. The Queen herself accepted

45 The coronation procession of Louis XV outside Rheims Cathedral, 1722

At various dates in the sixteenth, seventeenth and eighteenth centuries, most of the major and many of the minor powers of Europe adopted the form of government known as absolutism – that is, a form of hereditary monarchy in which the monarch was held to derive his power from God, was seen as the representative of God on earth and, most conspicuously in France in the reign of Louis XIV, was credited with semi-divine attributes. In the words of Bossuet: 'Consider the prince in his cabinet. From there issue the orders which set in motion together the magistrates and the captains, the citizens and the soldiers, the provinces and the armies by sea and land. This is the image of God who seated on His throne in the highest heavens sets the whole of nature in motion.'[27]

46 Jacques-Bénigne Bossuet (1627–1704), theologian and preacher, descended from a provincial Robe family. Here he is shown as Bishop of Meaux which he became in 1681. From 1670 Bossuet was tutor to the Dauphin whom he instructed in the duties as well as the rights of the monarchy

In the absolute monarchies of the Continent, the monarch alone had the right to make positive law, with the corollary that he could dispense his subjects from its operation. He did not have to render an account of his actions to any earthly authority. Resistance to him was seen as resistance to God Himself. While he was not accountable to his subjects, and while the law recognized no limitations in his power, it was always stressed, however, that he was accountable to God, that he was morally bound by the laws of God, and that he was similarly bound by the laws and customs of his kingdom because these were held to have the divine sanction. Contemporaries in England in the sixteenth century, and in France up to the middle of the eighteenth, always distinguished his rule from despotism, which

47 This is the classic image of the absolute monarch, representative of God on earth: Louis XIV by Hyacinthe Rigaud, 1701

they defined as arbitrary power, or power subject to no restrictions and therefore exercised out of relation to any principles. To quote Bossuet again: 'Kings are not absolved from [obedience to] the law.'[28] No two things can be more different 'than absolute government and arbitrary government'.[29]

The ideology of western absolutism, of which Bossuet was one of the more famous exponents, satisfied the needs of politically unsophisticated communities, which find comfort in the belief that their destinies are entrusted to a single all-powerful and yet beneficent being. The absolute monarch, like God Whom he represented on earth, was seen as the father of his people, to whom he owed justice tempered by mercy in return for unquestioning obedience. It had to

87

be recognized, of course, that the monarch, being human, might err, and that there could be bad kings, as there were bad fathers. When such misfortunes occurred, however, it was supposed that they had to be accepted as the will of God, against which it was not only impious but impolitic to rebel. The same kind of arguments that were used to justify parental authority, long after the absolute monarchies had vanished, were used earlier to justify the authority of the monarchs. Submission to even the worst monarch, it was said, was better than the anarchy, or the rule of a number of petty tyrants, which seemed the only alternatives. The fiction that parents must necessarily love and promote the interests of their children was maintained in relation to kings, as it was in relation to serf-owners and other hereditary wielders of authority. No father, it was continually pointed out, could wish to harm his children; no serf-owner could wish to harm the serfs on whom his prosperity depended. No monarch, for similar reasons, could wish to harm his subjects.

In the course of time, these assertions came to seem at variance with the facts. Because of a combination of causes that must be considered presently, the ideology of absolutism was undermined in one leading power after another in that period of its history here described as the Ancien Régime. It remained unchallenged, however, as long as the absolute monarchs seemed to provide more successful government than was to be had by other means.

When absolutism was in its prime the monarchs did this, particularly, because they were able to suppress all overt opposition by force, and by this means, though they could not ensure orderly government by modern standards, they could at least prevent civil war. On the Continent the absolute monarchs exercised their authority by means of their bureaucracies backed up by their standing armies, and it was on the latter that their authority rested in the last resort. The standing armies concentrated in the hands of the government a degree of force which it had never possessed before, and thereby made successful rebellion impossible, except in the single circumstance when the wielders of the force themselves became divided, or lacked the resolution to use it, as happened in France at the end of the 1780s.

48　*The Pack:* Gobelins tapestry from the famous series 'Louis XV's Hunts' by J. B. Oudry, 1743

In the primitive communities in which the absolute monarchs rose to power, absolutism in its prime thus proved itself superior to the other possible forms of government, by virtue of its ability to keep the peace at home and to mobilize men and money for national defence and aggrandizement. It also possessed potentialities, which in its earlier days the monarchs often exploited successfully, for increasing wealth, and thus for creating the economic conditions necessary for the waging of prolonged wars. Everywhere on the Continent the absolute monarchs attempted to foster trade and industry (and in Prussia also agriculture) by means of tariffs and subsidies. They subjected trade and industry to elaborate regulations and appointed officials to enforce them. On occasions they even engaged in these activities themselves, operating mines and factories: for example, the manufacture of the famous Gobelins tapestries in France. Everywhere they not only exercised a more or less minute control over the trades in grain, which in all countries were the most important domestic trades; they also maintained buffer stocks to act as a cushion against scarcity and famine, and by these and other means attempted to regulate grain prices. In Prussia in the time of Frederick the Great, when the government aimed at holding stocks equivalent to eighteen months' consumption, this feat was apparently accomplished with a remarkable degree of success.

49 This plate from the *Encyclopaedia* shows the high-warp technique of tapestry manufacture. The Gobelins factory still specializes in high-warp weaving

50 Louis XIV founded the Gobelins factory, and is here seen visiting it—an example of royal enterprise and the concern with fostering trade

Government intervention in economic matters worked more or less successfully in different times and places, but increasingly in the course of the eighteenth century in France, and later elsewhere, as the techniques of commerce and industry grew more sophisticated, it began to seem an impediment to progress. In the early days of absolutism, however, when most of the economies on the Continent were subject to natural disasters and stagnation, against which the efforts of individuals were impotent, the direction and capital investment which only a determined central authority was able to supply, could produce remarkable achievements. They did so most conspicuously in France in the time of Colbert and in Prussia in the reigns of Frederick William I and Frederick the Great.

51  Mme de Pompadour by François Boucher      52  Louis XV by Hyacinthe Rigaud, 1730

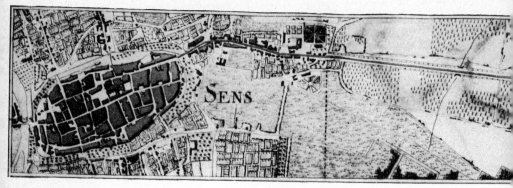

53 A surveyor's map of a portion of the route from Sens to Troyes, in the period 1768–86. Built by *corvée royale*, the route shown was called a *chemin* as distinct from a *grand' route*

In the eighteenth century – to the French, particularly – the establishment of absolute monarchy seemed to have ushered in a new and glorious chapter in their history. Indeed, it was regarded as responsible for the rebirth of civilization, which it was the fashion at the time to suppose had everywhere perished with the barbarian invasions. This, for example, was the principal theme of Voltaire's *Siècle de Louis XIV*. To Voltaire, as to most of his enlightened contemporaries, there could be no civilization without wealth, and no wealth without internal peace; and though Voltaire recognized that these blessings could be and had been achieved under other forms of government, he nevertheless also recognized that it was absolutism that had brought them to France, particularly in the early part of Louis XIV's reign. 'During nine hundred years', he said, 'the French genius was almost always cramped by a gothic government and by civil war and dissension. There were no fixed laws and customs; the language changed every other century but remained uncouth; the nobility was without discipline, knowing only war and idleness; the clergy lived in disorder and ignorance and the people without industry and sunk in misery.'[30] Though Voltaire admitted that Louis XIV had much to his discredit, and though there were people in enlightened circles, particularly Turgot, who thought that even so his eulogies went too far, nevertheless no theme was more common

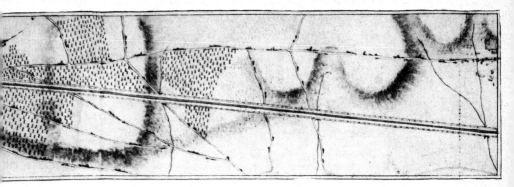

linking great towns. The sections shown are accompanied by notes taken annually by royal inspectors on the state of the roads

in the eighteenth century than that the Middle Ages, to quote the contemporary phrase, were 'gothic and barbarous', and that absolutism, in introducing an 'état policé' (by which was meant not a police state, but a state in which the central government maintained law and order), had made possible the growth of trade and industry, of the arts and sciences and of civilized living. Moreover, at the same time that the absolute monarchs had these achievements to their credit, the belief that they did not exercise their power arbitrarily seemed justified in the West by the respect they showed for custom.

The absolute monarchs exercised much wider powers than their predecessors, but they made no claims that their predecessors had not made in the past. They saw themselves as having triumphed over those who had tried to usurp their authority and not, after the fashion of the autocrats of more recent times, as having established a new form of government. They did not conceive of themselves as innovators, and could not indeed have done so, since the idea of change as either necessary or desirable was not generally acknowledged before the days of the Enlightenment, which first popularized this concept on the Continent. Whatever changes the absolute monarchs may have introduced in practice, in the West they never admitted to changing anything essential, but held themselves bound to observe the fundamental laws of their kingdoms.                    95

The doctrine of fundamental law, which was held in France in a form very similar to that in which it had been held in England in the sixteenth and early seventeenth centuries, provided the standard by which monarchy was distinguished from despotism. The so-called fundamental laws, or 'maxims', as they were sometimes described, were understood essentially as a body of principles in accordance with which government was supposed to proceed, and which in France, as early as the beginning of the seventeenth century, were spoken of as forming 'the constitution'.

In France, as in England before the Revolution of 1688, the fundamental laws were held to date back to time immemorial (for traditional societies prize things because they are old), and were seen as a manifestation of the law of nature and of reason, which God had implanted in the hearts of men. The Salic law, for example, which prevented women from inheriting the Crown, was defended in the sixteenth century on the grounds that it was 1200 years old (though in fact it dated only from the beginning of the fourteenth century); that it conformed to the law of nature 'which having created woman imperfect, and weak and feeble both in body and mind, has subjected her to the power of man'; and that sanction for it was to be found in the Book of Isaiah, Chapter Three, where 'God threatens his enemies with giving them women to rule over them as an insupportable malediction'.[31] As this illustration demonstrates, the belief in fundamental law was a belief by means of which the traditional societies of the West rationalized their respect for tradition.

Because the fundamental laws were seen as an expression of the law of nature, of reason, and of the will of God, it was held to be part of the monarch's Christian duties to observe them. In practice, however, this obligation may seem at first sight to have been without significance, since in any usual sense of the term the fundamental laws were not laws at all. In France, as in England, no list of them was ever made and there was no court with the acknowledged right to interpret them. Though in France the Parlements claimed this right, and saw their principal function in its exercise, no monarch ever admitted that he was bound by their judgements. It was generally accepted that royal decrees did not have the force of law until the

54 Engraving from the *Encyclopaedia* showing a canal with locks. The admiration excited by these inventions was expressed by the words in which the Emperor Joseph II wrote of the Canal of Picardy, in 1781: 'I am proud to be a man when I see that one of my fellow-creatures has dared to imagine and execute so bold and vast a work'

Parlements had registered them, and that the Parlements might remonstrate against any measures which the Crown proposed and which seemed to them unconstitutional. Every monarch, however, always maintained, and in the first half of the eighteenth century the Parlements commonly admitted, that, having listened to their remonstrances, he might override them if he saw fit, and he very frequently did so.

In these circumstances there was obviously no means of knowing in detail what the fundamental laws were. Their only significance was that they acted as a barrier against change. Though on most occasions it was impossible to agree whether or not any course of action contravened them, any clearly revolutionary action, such as abolishing a major institution of state or the privilege of important groups, plainly did so.

While these so-called fundamental laws therefore exercised no restraint on the day-to-day conduct of administration, they exercised considerable restraint on any desires the monarchs might have to introduce major changes, for the beliefs they symbolized were ones from which the monarchs in the West were no more emancipated than their subjects. Every monarch was brought up to believe that he must respect the fundamental laws and that if he did not do so, even though his subjects had no right of resistance, he incurred the wrath of God and could be labelled a despot.

Consequently in France, as in England under the Tudors, the monarchs changed as little as they could consistently with achieving their objectives. They did not destroy institutions or proscribe groups of people, apart from heretics, who were in a special position since they were outside the community of the faithful whom the king by his coronation oath was pledged to defend. They might deal harshly with individuals who stood in their path, for it was not until the days of the Enlightenment that the individual as such was held to have inherent rights. But in principle they always respected the rights of groups, which they attacked, and then with circumspection, only when these menaced their authority.

The French monarchs, like the Tudors, thus left the old institutions standing while creating new ones more immediately under

55 The Intendances and Pays d'Etat of France in 1789

their control. The most conspicuous example of this practice in France was the appointment of the *Intendants de province*, whose office first became permanent at the beginning of Louis XIV's reign. The *Intendants* were the king's representatives in the provinces, and, like the ministers, they did not buy their offices in perpetuity but

99

were directly appointed by the Crown. Their official title was that of 'commissars dispatched to execute the king's orders', and as such, among their other powers, they were given authority to watch and report on the way in which the holders of the old established and venal offices, particularly the magistrates of the Parlements, discharged their duties. Often they were authorized by special commissions to take over these duties themselves. At the time they were appointed, their principal functions were, on the one hand, to raise money for the Crown, but on the other, to maintain order and justice, to prevent corruption and the intimidation of the weak by the strong and in general to promote the prosperity of the provinces for which they were responsible. The Scotsman, John Law, famous for having inaugurated in France the equivalent of the South Sea Bubble, once observed to the Marquis d'Argenson: 'Monsieur, I would never have believed what I discovered when I was in control of the finances. You should know that this kingdom of France is ruled by thirty *Intendants*. You have neither Parlements . . . nor Estates, nor Governors, I might almost add neither king nor ministers, but thirty [men] . . . on whom depends the welfare or the misery of the provinces. . . .'[32]

56, 57 Two *Intendants*: Louis, Marquis de Tourny, *Intendant* of Limoges (1730) and then of Guyenne (1743); and Antoine-Martin, Chaumont de la Galaizières, *Intendant* of Alsace-Lorraine (1737)

58 Henri-François Daguesseau (1668–1751), one of the famous chancellors of France, noted for his learning and integrity. Though a member of a provincial Robe family his grand-daughter married the Duc de Noailles. Her grandson was the famous Marquis de Lafayette

This often-quoted statement was nevertheless an exaggeration. The Parlements, the Estates and the provincial Governors, who had lorded it in the provinces before the days of the *Intendants*, continued to exist and, in the latter part of the eighteenth century, regained much of their former power. The authority of the *Intendants*, which was never precisely defined, varied in different periods according to the extent to which the king was prepared to back it up. In many parts of France, even in Louis XIV's day, it had not been supreme. Writing of the *Intendance* of Brittany, where there were both a Parlement and provincial Estates, Henry Freville said of the first permanent *Intendant*, appointed in 1689, that he was 'not the only representative of the monarchy and was never to become so'.[33] Louis XV's famous chancellor, Daguesseau, used to tell his children that their grandfather, who was *Intendant* of Languedoc, 'realized from the start that the welfare of the province depended principally on a perfect harmony between the three principal persons who provided, as it were, the soul and motive force of the state – the Governor, the *Intendant* and the President of the Estates'.[34]

It was this sort of situation which Montesquieu had in mind when he defended the privileges of groups as part of the fundamental law of France and saw in them, as was shown earlier, a barrier against despotism. To Montesquieu an essential characteristic of absolute monarchy was that it permitted the existence of 'intermediate powers'; and this, in his view, distinguished it from despotism, in which the concept of fundamental law was unknown and the arbitrary will of the ruler in consequence supreme. Monarchy, Montesquieu said, allowed for adjustments, discussion and remonstrances, whereas under despotism there was only the naked exercise of power. The despot recognized no privilege and so made a sense of honour impossible. He reduced all men to the position of equals in slavery, so that they became servile, corrupt and incapable of magnanimity. Under despotism, as he put it, 'l'homme est une créature qui obéit à une créature qui veut' – man is a creature who obeys another creature who wills.

Montesquieu nevertheless admitted that although absolute monarchs exacted obedience in a different way from despots, the nature of their power was the same, since both the monarch and the despot were alike absolved from rendering an account of their actions to anyone and from any legal limitations on the exercise of their will.

'The whole difference', Montesquieu said in one place, between monarchy and despotism is that 'in a monarchy the prince is a person of understanding, and his ministers are infinitely more skilful and experienced than they are in despotically governed states'.[35]

As he expressed it in this passage, Montesquieu's criterion for distinguishing between monarchy and despotism was a nebulous one, like the concept of fundamental law on which he based it. Who was to say, for example, whether Louis XIV had sufficient understanding, and his ministers sufficient skill and experience, to escape the charge of despotism? Different people answered this question differently in Louis' lifetime as different historians, and even the same historians on different occasions, have done since. There were, however, circumstances in which the criterion served to mark an important distinction.

It was the fashion in France in the eighteenth century to contrast the monarchies of the West with the despotisms of the Orient and the Middle East, and particularly with the Turkish despotism. The strictures made on the latter were often misinformed. Yet much that was said about them was true, and applicable in varying degrees to the monarchies in central and eastern Europe, which it nevertheless usually seemed inappropriate to criticize in public, because the worst offenders – the Prussian and the Russian monarchs – paid lip-service to enlightened ideas in the second half of the eighteenth century, gave sanctuary to the enlightened writers when they were forced to fly from France, and called them in as advisers. In spite of this, the Russian monarchy, before the accession of Catherine the Great and to a large extent even afterwards, differed very markedly from the French, and in a way that nothing illuminates so well as Montesquieu's distinction between absolutism and despotism. The same, though with important qualifications, could be said of the Prussian monarchy.

The course of Russian history before the eighteenth century had been entirely different from that of the West. In the Middle Ages many causes, and especially the absence of opposition from a powerful church and powerful towns, had combined to give the Tsars an undisputed authority such as no Western monarchs had ever enjoyed. The Tsars were restrained by no belief in the virtue of custom and privilege, but were accustomed to tear up their institutions by the roots when the mood seized them. Just as the peasants had no rights against the landlords, so the landlords had no rights or even any recognized claims against the Tsar. Peter the Great tortured and murdered them with his own hands. 'Near the Tsar near death', it was said in his day, and this remained true for long afterwards. By the famous charter of the nobility of 1785, Catherine the Great gave the nobility thirty-six rights, many of which – for example, immunity from corporal punishment – had been enjoyed by nobles in the West since time immemorial. It was only at this time, and then with many qualifications, that what was understood by civilization in the West began to penetrate into the Russian upper classes. In its ignorance of the very idea of human dignity, in its violence, lawlessness and brutality, in its widespread use of obscene tortures and, above all, in its lack of privileged groups, Russia, throughout most of the eighteenth century, conformed exactly to Montesquieu's idea of what he called a 'monstrous government'.

The Prussian government did not conform to Montesquieu's criterion to the same extent, but it did so in many ways in the time of Frederick William I, and in a number of ways even in the time of Frederick the Great. Frederick William I, in the course of his many fits of rage against his officials, used to say that he would 'hang and roast', like the Tsar, 'singe and burn', and inflict 'exemplary punishment in good Russian fashion'.[36] He did not carry out his threats but it was significant that he could make them. In his reign, and in the reign of his son, not only did the despotism of the landlord, as in Russia, weigh heavily on the serf, but the despotism of the 'autocrat', as both the Prussian and Russian monarchs were described, weighed

59  Catherine the Great (Tsarina Catherine II) walking her dog at Tsarskoye Selo

60 Frederick the Great
of Brandenburg-Prussia
(1712–86)

heavily on his officials. While in Prussia, as in Russia, the monarchs
left the landowners a large discretion to tyrannize over their serfs,
they themselves showed little more respect for human dignity (and
Frederick the Great showed less than Catherine) in the way they
treated those landowners who entered the royal service. Any Prussian
official in Frederick's day might immediately find himself in Spandau,
the Prussian equivalent of the Bastille, and condemned to menial
tasks, no matter how exalted his rank, if he dared so much as to
question the appropriateness of the royal commands. The Prussian
government, for all its merits (under Frederick it was the least
disorderly, inefficient and dishonest government in Europe), left no
place for the discussions, adjustments and remonstrances dear to the
heart of Montesquieu, and little for honour as it was understood in
France. To Mirabeau, notwithstanding his admiration for Frederick
personally, it seemed an intolerable despotism, as it did to other
visitors from the West.

105

Montesquieu's distinction thus corresponded to certain realities in the Europe of his day, and yet it increasingly grew to seem unimportant in France. It paled into insignificance by comparison with the new criteria the British had established for themselves in the seventeenth century, and which indeed Montesquieu himself in certain respects endorsed and even added to in some chapters of *De l'Esprit des Lois*.

According to these criteria, any government was arbitrary, or despotic, unless it observed the rule of law and guaranteed certain specific rights to the individual. By the rule of law was understood, in particular, that all citizens in the same circumstances should be tried by the same law, regardless of religion, birth or status; that no government servant should take any action in the discharge of his official functions unless he was authorized to do so by some specific law; that the law should be interpreted by judges chosen for their skill and experience and immune from political influence; and that it should be binding on the government until such time as it was changed in accordance with the recognized procedure.

By the rights of the individual were understood, in particular, the right not to be imprisoned without cause shown, or kept in prison for any length of time without trial; the right to trial by jury in criminal cases; the right to security of property under the law; the right, with certain qualifications, to freedom of speech, of the press and of worship.

The British believed that the prerequisite of all these conditions was that the government should be accountable to an elected assembly, whose consent should be necessary to the making of law, because, as the first Lord Halifax, commonly known as 'the Trimmer', once observed: 'To say that a power is supreme and not arbitrary is not sense.'[37]

All these principles were as alien to the principles of the French monarchy as they were to those of the other Continental monarchies. Privilege, in its original sense of special rights guaranteed to particular groups, was the antithesis of the first condition of the rule of law. The belief that the king alone made positive law and might dispense his subjects from its operations, meant, among other things, that he might, when he chose, grant large discretionary powers to his servants, as the French kings did to the *Intendants*. It also meant that the judges, so far from being immune from government influence, were seen, in Bacon's words, as 'lions under the throne' whose principal duty was to enforce the rights of the Crown, and that, even so, the king might remove cases from their competence and require them to be tried by particular individuals or by *ad hoc* commissions whose members were specially chosen for the occasion.

As has already been pointed out, the French absolute monarchs did not recognize the rights of the individual. Though they paid some, and indeed an increasing, amount of lip-service to the rights of property, they denied the rights of freedom of speech, of the press and of worship. Like the monarchs of the other leading powers, they maintained their secret police, though it was less ubiquitous and efficient than in Prussia and in the Habsburg dominions under Joseph II, and they threw people into prison without trial and kept them there indefinitely.

On various occasions in the course of their careers, most of the famous writers of the Enlightenment became the victims of these practices, though not on a scale sufficient to prevent them from saying most of what they wanted or to arrest the dissemination of their opinions. Though political offences were punished by arbitrary imprisonment in France, they were punished less effectively and with less determination than in the other major powers, because the principal supporters of the new ideas were members or protégés of the ruling class itself. The most numerous class of persons who found their way without trial into the Bastille, Vincennes, Bicêtre, and other prisons, were men such as Monnerat, whose cause Malesherbes made famous in 1770, and who spent twenty months in a dungeon, on the mere, and unfounded, suspicion of having infringed the regulations of the tax-farm. But they also included the victims, as Malesherbes put it, of 'private passions', particularly the members of families whose relations found them troublesome, and who, on the grounds that they jeopardized the family honour, could get them locked up by procuring *lettres de cachet*, which were doled out, in the reign of Louis XV, like blank cheques, to ministers and other officials,

Mons. de Bernaville, je vous escris cette lettre de l'avis de mon Oncle le Duc d'Orleans Regent, pour vous dire que mon intention est que vous receuiez dans mon Chasteau de la Bastille le S.ʳ ... et que vous l'y deteniez jusqu'à nouvel ordre, Sur ce je prie Dieu qu'il vous ayt Mons. de Bernaville en sa S.ᵗᵉ garde. Escrit à Paris le 17. May 1717.

Louis

who then filled in the names of the people they, or their friends, wanted to imprison.

Voltaire dedicated his novel *L'ingénu* to these various classes of unfortunates. He portrayed *l'ingénu* as the member of a tribe of North American Indians, the Hurons, whose habits we now know to have been peculiarly disgusting and uncivilizable, but from whom he nevertheless chose this representative of the 'noble savage'. *L'ingénu*, he tells us, landed in Brittany in 1689 and immediately came to the help of the inhabitants who were engaged in driving off a British raiding party. He was advised to go to Versailles to claim a reward from the king, but on the way he fell in with a party of Huguenot refugees with whom he commiserated, and as a result found himself in the Bastille.

While in prison, like many others of Voltaire's heroes, he 'fortified' his reason by reflection, and this moved him on one occasion to

61, 62 Left, *lettre de cachet* of 1717, ordering Voltaire to be imprisoned in the Bastille (where he remained for eleven months). Right, plan of the elevation of the Bastille

exclaim to the prisoner who shared his cell: 'We are both of us in irons without knowing who is responsible and without even being able to ask. I lived as a Huron for twenty years. They are said to be barbarians because they take vengeance on their enemies, but they have never oppressed their friends. I had scarcely set foot in France when I shed my blood for her. As a reward I am buried in this living tomb. . . . Are there then no laws in this country? They condemn men without a hearing. It is not so in England. Ah! it was not against England that I should have fought.'[38]

By 1767, when Voltaire's Swiss publisher, Cramer, first brought out *L'ingénu*, these views were already common and they gathered force with the years. On the eve of the Revolution, when the French people assembled to draw up their *cahiers de doléances*, or list of grievances, the complaint that the French government was a despotism was universal.

63 Nicolas-René Berryer,
Lieutenant General
of police (1747–57),
Minister of Marine
(1758–61)

It was not, however, based on the old argument that custom had been overridden, but on the new criteria evolved by the British. At this time, Britain's attempt to keep the American colonies in subjection, as well as her failure to do so, had greatly diminished French respect for her. By 1789, because of the corruption of her political system and the concentration of power in the hands of the aristocracy, it was widely believed in France that England did not deserve to be called a free country. Everyone, however, including Sieyès who detested her, had come to accept her definition of arbitrary power. The belief in fundamental law as a barrier against arbitrariness went the same way as it had gone in England a hundred years earlier. Halifax, who died in 1695, observed at some unrecorded date, 'Every party, when they find a maxim for their turn, they presently call it a fundamental.'[39] Rabaut Saint-Étienne, writing on the eve of the Revolution, held the same opinion. 'They tell you', he said, 'of the monarchical constitution, of the ancient maxims of the monarchy, of the fundamental laws of the monarchy: these are only empty words.'[40]

Though the French in the second half of the eighteenth century, however, came to believe increasingly that their government acted despotically, they did not believe that the king himself was a despot. The phrase on everyone's lips, repeated in every *cahier*, was 'le despotisme ministeriel' – the despotism of the ministers.

In politically unsophisticated communities, ruled by some form of autocracy, it has always been common to exonerate the ruler from blame for any misfortunes that may befall the community, and to lay the blame on his servants. This way of arguing was, however, a proof (which came to be recognized sooner or later in every absolute monarchy) that the king's supreme power was, except in a purely legal sense, as much of a myth as his being bound by the law. As de Maistre put it in the nineteenth century, 'nothing is further from the truth than that the will of the monarch is personally responsible for everything. . . . Human power creates its own limits, it destroys itself by the very efforts it makes to extend itself. Up to a certain point the more one increases the dimensions of a telescope, or of a firearm, the greater its effectiveness, but if this point is passed, the effectiveness begins to diminish by huge proportions.'[41]

64 Chrétien-Guillaume de Lamoignon de Malesherbes (1721–94), an ancestor of Tocqueville, was born of a distinguished Robe family that had married into ducal houses. A friend of the Philosophes, he protected them when he was appointed chief censor (1750–63), and as Premier Président of the Cour des Aides he fulminated against the issue of *lettres de cachet* and other acts of despotism

Even in the heyday of the absolute monarchs, their power was subject to much greater limitations than is often supposed. Their reputedly centralized bureaucracies were centralized only in the sense that power was exercised everywhere by royal officials, except in the serf-owning countries where, for most purposes, it stopped, in practice if not in theory, at the gates of the manor. The bureaucracies were never centralized in the sense that it was possible, except in the broadest general terms, to lay down at the centre the policy that was to be pursued in the provinces. Apart from any other reasons, communications were too bad and laws, customs and privileges too diverse, to make possible centralized control, as it is now understood.

The power of the absolute monarchs was limited, in the first place, by their ignorance of what it was practicable to demand, so that a large degree of discretion had to be left to the people on the spot. It was further limited by their ignorance of the policies which their servants, who usually had an interest in deceiving them, pursued at the centre as well as locally. Louis XIV, as Lavisse tells us in what is still the standard account of his reign, was never informed of the atrocities committed against the Huguenots, although he was renowned, by comparison with his successors, for the seriousness with which he took affairs of state. Frederick the Great had an easier task than the French kings because his population was much smaller – it was only $2\frac{1}{4}$ million at his accession and about 5 million at his death – and because many duties, which devolved in France on the royal officials, were left in Prussia to the serf-owners. Even so, as Professor Hans Rosenberg writes, Frederick's officials 'effectively contrived' to block 'the enforcement of the royal regulations if they saw fit to do so'.[42] Indeed, an eminent contemporary Prussian bureaucrat, Benckendorf, himself once observed that these regulations 'are drafted, printed, published, but rarely obeyed'.[43]

Frederick the Great had a capacity far above the average for administration and sustained work. In these respects he was proverbially an exception among the crowned heads of Europe. In the ordinary course of events, the power of the absolute monarchs, besides being limited in the ways already described, was also limited by their defects of character and intellect. Although in the age of

65 Maria Theresa and her family on the terrace of Schönbrunn, Francis I is seated on the left, the young Joseph, heir to the throne, stands in the centre of the star pattern

absolutism there were monarchs with remarkable qualities of courage and common sense (Maria Theresa, for example) and a few, notably Frederick the Great, of remarkable intelligence, the normal operations of heredity ensured that in general their intelligences were only mediocre, and sometimes below average. Besides, their education, once they had ceased to be personally responsible for military operations and for leading their armies in battle, deprived them, as the Prussian field-marshal, von Boyen, pointed out, of the knowledge of any class of people except courtiers, and the experience of many essential problems of government. Louis XIV himself admitted that he did not understand financial matters, though an understanding of them was vital. The efforts of Calonne to instruct Louis XVI on the nature of the French government debt would be laughable but for the tragic consequences.

There was thus an inherent contradiction in the nature of absolutism, which became increasingly apparent as the tasks of government became more complicated, and which led to no serious consequences only so long as the absolute monarchies were not brought into competition with more efficient forms of government. On the one hand, the power of the absolute monarch was proclaimed to be supreme, subject to his moral obligation to observe the fundamental laws; and this was always interpreted to mean that he could when he chose interfere in matters of administration. But on the other hand, the instrument of his power was his bureaucracy, and bureaucracies, if they are to discharge their duties in an orderly way, must work according to rules, and by means of a recognized chain of command, without which officials cannot be expected to show the loyalty and sense of responsibility that are essential to proper functioning.

Because of the experience of their predecessors and often, too, from a sense of their own inadequacies, the absolute monarchs were jealous of their authority. They could never tolerate a first minister, in the sense of a minister with a recognized authority over his colleagues and a recognized responsibility for formulating policy; for as the experience of Richelieu, in particular, had shown, ministers in this position usurped the power and patronage of the king himself.

This state of affairs had the result, in the first place, that the monarch's policy towards his servants was commonly governed by the principle of divide and rule. Louis XIV once said: 'I wished to entrust my orders to a number of people in order to concentrate authority in my hands alone.'[44] The monarchs encouraged and even required their principal servants to spy on each other. They duplicated offices for this purpose and, in France, to make money from their sale as well. In Prussia under Frederick the Great, and in the hereditary lands of the House of Habsburg under Joseph II, the secret police was a weapon devised rather for use by the monarch against his officials than by the government against the public.

In the second place, the determination of the monarch to keep power in his own hands meant that he acknowledged no restrictions on the sources from which he took advice. In France as in England,

66 The Habsburg emperor, Joseph II, and his younger brother Leopold II, Grand Duke of Tuscany, in Rome, 1769

in the early days of absolutism, the monarchs had been accustomed on important occasions to consult a council composed of their principal officials. As this procedure proved too cumbersome and restrictive, they then had recourse to small committees, whose members they chose from the principal office-holders. They did not, however, feel themselves bound to consult only these men. They commonly discussed affairs of state with their wives, mistresses, and other people without official functions who often gained domination over them.

In Prussia, where Frederick William I and Frederick the Great always kept before their eyes the example of French policy steered into disastrous courses by bad advice, there emerged the unique institution known to the Germans as 'cabinet government'. This was, however, the opposite of what is understood by that term in Britain, since it was designed to ensure that the monarch, when making up his mind, was protected from all external influences, and particularly from what the eighteenth-century Hohenzollerns called 'raisonieren', or argument, which seemed incompatible with their autocracy. 115

Frederick the Great, in his cabinet in Potsdam, communicated with his officials in Berlin by means of four secretaries, whom he described as his clerks. The officials, whom he ordinarily never saw, reported to him in writing. In the long run, however, this arrangement was no more capable than the methods resorted to elsewhere of keeping power in the hands of monarchs who, because of their temperaments and training, and the growing complexity of government business, were incapable of exercising it. In the reign of Frederick William III the people principally responsible for Prussian policy were the cabinet secretaries, by this time known as the cabinet ministers, against whom von Stein launched a famous indictment in 1806. He held cabinet government to have been the chief cause of Prussia's military defeats because, as he put it, the cabinet ministers 'have all the power, make all the decisions, fill all the posts, but have no responsibility,' while those with whom responsibility rested were unable to influence decisions and so lost their sense of duty and self-respect. 'It is essential', Stein said, 'that a direct link should be re-established between the king and his chief officials; that the people who bring matters before the king for his final decision should be recognized as having this duty and should be entrusted with it by law; that their meetings should be organized in a way that will serve the purpose and that they should be held responsible for their decisions.'[45]

Long before these problems arose to perplex the Prussians, they had been recognized in other parts of Europe. The need to unite power and responsibility; the need to fix responsibility; the need to organize the work of government and administration in accordance with rationally devised principles – these had come to seem increasingly urgent in the second half of the eighteenth century, and particularly, among the leading powers, in France and the Habsburg dominions, which were the victims of military defeat. Above all in France, which, among the leading powers, had by far the most highly developed urban economy and, apart from Russia, the largest population, absolutism and the privileged society, increasingly recognized as two sides of the same medal, were plainly reducing administration to chaos.

Because there was no machinery for co-ordinating the actions of ministers, they proceeded, as Necker once observed, like the heads of sovereign states at war with each other. Because the powers of no authorities were precisely defined, and could be interfered with by the monarchs at their good pleasure on the advice of whoever gained their confidence, there were continual conflicts of jurisdiction. Because as a matter of principle the monarchs set all their servants at loggerheads by encouraging them to spy on each other, and because there was no established routine for presenting matters for the monarch's decision, he was continually bombarded by contradictory opinions on matters which increasingly became too complicated for him to understand. As a result no consistent line of policy could ever be formulated. Until just before the Revolution, when provincial assemblies were set up, no consultation of any section of the population was permitted, and yet at the same time the monarchs were afraid of being accused of despotic action if they introduced changes by force; consequently no course of action could be embarked on which seemed likely to arouse serious opposition. The innumerable legal privileges which clogged the wheels of government at every turn had therefore to be left standing, whether they were the privileges of the village communities which stood in the way of agricultural reform, or the tax privileges of nobles, bourgeois, clerics, *pays d'états* and other bodies, which made it impossible to assess or collect the taxes in a rational way.

Thus absolute monarchy, which had seemed in its prime to be the strongest form of government, seemed distinguished in its decline principally by its weakness. In France, and later elsewhere, it came to be thought synonymous with arbitrary power, not only in the sense in which that term had been used in England under the Stuarts, when it meant the violation of the rights of the individual, but also in the wider sense that administration proceeded out of relation to any rules or principles. The third estate of Nemours complained in 1789 that there was no law or privilege, 'the limits and extent of which are precisely known'.[46] Pierre Champion, in his *La France d'après les Cahiers de 1789*, written in 1911, said that 'to believe in such a degree of anarchy, or even to imagine it, it is necessary to make the difficult effort of renouncing all the habits of precision contracted during the past hundred years'.[47]

It is often said that this state of affairs was due to the accident that Louis XIV's successors lacked his sense of duty and firmness of purpose. This explanation is plainly inadequate, since sooner or later comparable conditions arose in every absolute monarchy and the last absolute monarchs in the leading powers usually showed similar characteristics. The incompetence, indecisiveness and lack of loyalty to their servants, for which most of them are notorious, were the natural consequences of difficulties which their predecessors had not experienced. The tasks and the machinery of government increasingly grew more complicated and thus eluded their comprehension and control. The kind of rational approach to social and political problems for which the Enlightenment was responsible, undermined belief in the 'divinity that doth hedge a king'.

This combination of causes dispelled the two myths on which the ideology of Western absolutism had been based. Not only did it become plain that the government was not bound by the law and that its power was arbitrary; it also became plain that, except in a purely legal sense, the monarch's supreme power was an illusion, and that the lack of any recognized and deliberately devised restraints on it had served merely to recreate in a new form the very situation for which absolutism had once provided a remedy. French historians often refer to the 'administrative feudalism' of the Ancien Régime, by which they mean that dispersal of authority among ministers and other authorities, such as the tax-farmers, which contemporaries had in mind when they spoke of 'ministerial despotism'.

# III THE DYNAMIC OF CHANGE

The Ancien Régime had inherited from the Middle Ages a set of values which extolled the military and Christian virtues – courage, austerity, devotion and self-sacrifice – in a way that made Army and Church complementary professions of parallel and equal dignity. These values found their supreme expression in the waging of war. As it was expressed by the Baron de Besenval, the commander of the king's Swiss Guard, 'La guerre est une passion' – war is a passion; 'but for this, how could a man decide to leave a comfortable life to expose himself to continual vexations . . . to hunger, to thirst, to fatigue . . . to the necessity of forgetting himself for others and to mutilating wounds?'[1] This ideal was sanctified in Prussia by Frederick the Great's victories, and survived to demonstrate its power in the Germany of a much later period. In eighteenth-century France it was already weakening. Besenval himself, after exalting the military virtues, concluded that if he were asked to choose between 'the great tragic scenes' and 'the peace of our century', he would prefer the latter.

His words, however, do not carry much conviction. Noted for his success in the *salons* and his collection of *objets d'art* in his latter years, but for his exploits of military daring in his youth, he wrote with more eloquence of the arts of war than of the arts of peace. He was one of those who, in Voltaire's words, had a civil war in his soul, and his ambivalent attitude was typical of his class.

Faced with the decline in French military power, many aristocrats looked for a remedy not to social change but to a return to the old values which, they supposed, money had corrupted. They were prepared to make more concessions to the new values than is sometimes admitted. By 1789, all were willing to give up their privileges in matters of taxation. But they were not prepared to give up their

67, 68 Military figures: Pierre-Victor, Baron de Bésenval (left), commander of the King's Swiss Guard in 1789, courtier and memoir-writer; and Louis II de Bourbon, Prince de Condé, the famous general of Louis XIV's reign

honorific privileges, including their right to sit separately from the Third Estate in the States General – for these were the badges of their order guaranteed them by law. They clung to the myths of blood and of the nobility as an estate; and they did so because they believed, as Miromesnil kept tediously repeating in his debate with Turgot over the abolition of the *corvée*, staged for the instruction of Louis XVI in 1776, that it was to these that France had owed her greatness.

It was this conception of military virtue, and of victory in war as the basis of French civilization, which was challenged in the middle of the eighteenth century by the writers of the Enlightenment commonly known as the 'Philosophes'.

69 Duc de Rohan-Soubise (1715–87), Marshal of France, here portrayed as the colonel of the Régiment de Soubise. He was notorious as the Commander-in-chief of the army of French and German troops which Frederick the Great, with much inferior numbers, put to flight at the battle of Rossbach in 1757

70 Hermann-Maurice, Comte de Saxe, was the illegitimate son of Augustus II, Elector of Saxony and King of Poland, and of the Countess Aurore of Koenigsmark. He became one of the most distinguished field-marshals of his time, and conquered the Spanish Low Countries in the War of the Austrian Succession

71 Armand-Thomas-Hue de Miromesnil (1723–96), Président of the Rouen Parlement in 1757, Keeper of the Seals, 1774–87. An enemy of the Philosophes and Turgot's opponent in the debate over the abolition of the *corvée* (*see p. 120*)

In the second half of the eighteenth century, enlightened ideas gained currency all over Europe, but their source was in France. Yet the French have no word for the Enlightenment. They can only refer to it as 'le siècle des lumières', or the century of light. This translation, however, fails to convey the meaning of the French term, which is one that is no longer used. For when, in the eighteenth century, one spoke of 'les lumières' one meant, as Turgot once wrote in a letter to Hume, the capacity to see to the 'true causes' of things. In his *Considérations sur les Mœurs*, Duclos defined the spirit of Enlightment as a way of thinking, the reverse of conventional, that did not proceed by deduction from accepted premises, but, by taking all possibly relevant circumstances into account, established connections between phenomena that had previously appeared unrelated, and so arrived at new and more profound explanations. Enlightenment thus meant not knowledge or intelligence, though these were necessary to it, but insight and understanding and, in this sense, illumination.

72, 73 Antoine Caritat, Marquis de Condorcet (1743–94), a distinguished mathematician and one of the more radical Philosophes, became President of the Legislative Assembly at the time of the Revolution. His rich wife brought him the Château de Villette at Condécourt (left). He committed suicide under the Terror to escape execution

The Philosophes believed that enlightenment had been vouchsafed to them by the discoveries of the seventeenth century, particularly those of Newton, which had illuminated the nature of the material universe, and those of Locke, which had done the same for the human mind. They were a body of professional writers, philosophizers for the great part rather than philosophers, whom Condorcet once described as 'a class of men less concerned with discovering truth than with propagating it', who 'find their glory rather in destroying popular error than in pushing back the frontiers of knowledge'.[2] Their great enterprise, the *Encyclopaedia*, whose seventeen volumes came out, after various unfortunate encounters with the censorship, between 1751 and 1765, was devoted to this task. A vehicle for propaganda as much as for disseminating knowledge, it set out to familiarize the layman with the new discoveries in science, and with the kind of rational thinking of which they were the fruit. By this means, it strove to inculcate a critical approach to

123

the problems of human relationships and, as Condorcet said, to track down 'prejudice in those sheltered places where the Clergy, the Government and the ancient corporations are protecting it'.[3] Their ultimate purpose was to spread the belief that human behaviour, like the material universe, was amenable to scientific investigation, and that society and government should be studied scientifically in the interests of human happiness.

Within the scope of this short essay it would be impossible to consider the implications of this great intellectual movement, which laid the foundations of the social sciences of psychology, anthropology, sociology and economics, and provided liberals, Socialists and finally Communists, with their inspiration – Marx, for example, said that Diderot was his favourite reading, and Trotsky was greatly influenced by Condorcet. Here the Enlightenment can be considered only as a solvent of the old order. It proved a potent one, because it provided all the discontented with principles by which to justify their discontents and with visions of a better future to inspire the attempts at change.

74, 75, 76 Denis Diderot (1713–84, far left), the son of a master cutler, one of the most distinguished thinkers of the Enlightenment and principal editor of the *Encyclopaedia*. His co-editor was Jean-Le-Rond d'Alembert (left), a noted mathematician, the illegitimate child of Mme de Tencin and the Chevalier Détouches-Carron. D'Alembert was found abandoned on the steps of the Church of St-Jean-Le-Rond from which he derived his Christian name. Right, title-page of the first volume, 1751

# ENCYCLOPÉDIE,

## OU

# DICTIONNAIRE RAISONNÉ

# DES SCIENCES,

## DES ARTS ET DES MÉTIERS,

### PAR UNE SOCIÉTÉ DE GENS DE LETTRES.

Mis en ordre & publié par M. *DIDEROT*, de l'Académie Royale des Sciences & des Belles-Lettres de Pruſſe; & quant à la PARTIE MATHÉMATIQUE, par M. *D'ALEMBERT*, de l'Académie Royale des Sciences de Paris, de celle de Pruſſe, & de la Société Royale de Londres.

*Tantùm ſeries junĉturaque pollet,*
*Tantùm de medio ſumptis accedit honoris !* HORAT.

## TOME PREMIER.

### A PARIS,

Chez {
BRIASSON, *rue Saint Jacques, à la Science.*
DAVID l'aîné, *rue Saint Jacques, à la Plume d'or.*
LE BRETON, Imprimeur ordinaire du Roy, *rue de la Harpe.*
DURAND, *rue Saint Jacques, à Saint Landry, & au Griffon.*
}

### M. DCC. LI.

*AVEC APPROBATION ET PRIVILEGE DU ROY.*

77, 78 Left, Jean-Jacques Rousseau (1712–78). Right, engraving from the *Encyclopaedia* to illustrate the article on anatomy

The teaching of the Philosophes on social and political questions was profoundly revolutionary, since they attacked all the assumptions on which the old order rested, held all existing institutions up to ridicule, and continually pointed out that society was rotten. On the other hand, their doctrines did not crystallize into a revolutionary creed until after the Ancien Régime had already begun to collapse under the impact of impending bankruptcy and the measures adopted to avert it.

The attempts that are now sometimes made to defend the Philosophes against the charge of Utopianism hardly stand up to investigation, since even when they did not, like Rousseau in his *Contrat Social*, concern themselves with the construction of Utopias, they always argued on the assumption that man was the creature of his environment, and that the propensities for evil which he only too obviously displayed could be diminished or eradicated if his environment were changed. None of them, however, ever concerned himself with the means by which power could be seized and used to bring this result about.

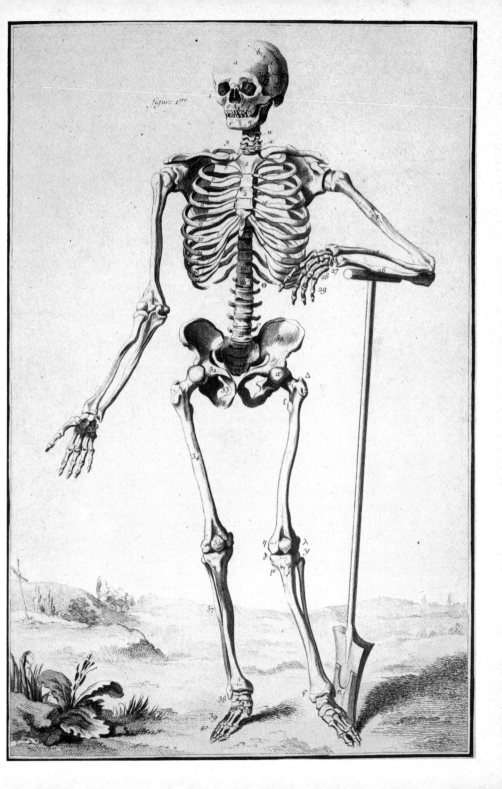

figure 1.re

Notwithstanding the revolutionary nature of their opinions, nothing was further from their minds than the idea of revolution, which, indeed, on the scale on which it occurred in 1789, was an unknown phenomenon. With the exception of Diderot (the only famous Philosophe, perhaps significantly, who could never bring himself to conform to the standards of behaviour required in the *salons*), theirs was not the stuff of which martyrs are made, nor was there any place in their creed for martyrdom. Seeing it as their principal task to undermine the habits of blind obedience to authority in Church and State, and to establish man's right to doubt, they extended their belief in reason to include reasonableness, and 'fanaticism' was the strongest term of abuse in their vocabulary. In consequence, when the Paris Parlement and the Sorbonne condemned Helvétius' *De l'Esprit* in 1759, Helvétius made a complete recantation, which Maupertuis, it is true, thought cowardly, but which Voltaire held to be only sensible, since it permitted Helvétius to continue his writing and to live, albeit in official exile, the life of a beneficent *grand seigneur* on his estates. In the same year, when the government suppressed the *Encyclopaedia*, its editor, Diderot, who was determined to carry on the work underground, found himself deserted by all his contributors.

These being their attitudes, the Philosophes founded no political parties and produced no schemes for reform. Untrammelled by the discipline that the need to translate a programme into action enforces, individually they allowed their ideas to develop with a remarkable disregard for consistency, and in conjunction produced ideas that, given the common assumptions from which they started, were to a remarkable degree incompatible one with another. Professor Talmon found in the Enlightenment the origins of totalitarian democracy. This outraged many of his readers, to whom the Philosophes stood essentially for liberalism. The two points of view, however, are not incompatible. If the essence of liberalism may be said to lie in the belief that the ultimate object of government action is to promote the happiness and dignity of the individual, and that the rule of law and civil liberties are necessary means to this end, then all the Philosophes were liberals. At the same time,

79 Claude-Adrien Helvétius (1715–71), General Farmer (1738–51), philanthropist and famous Philosophe, distinguished by his radicalism. His grandfather was a court doctor of Swiss origins who acquired French nobility in the reign of Louis XIV. He is seen here with his family

however, the traditions in which they had been educated, and the conditions in which they lived, compelled them to acknowledge aims and advocate measures which were not liberal.

This is particularly noticeable in their attitude towards happiness. They all assumed that happiness on earth was the ultimate good. This was an *idée fixe* in enlightened circles which seemed too obvious to need defence, and which involved denying both the Christian belief in purification through suffering and the belief of the privileged and militaristic societies in the heroic virtues. The Philosophes used the term, however, in two different senses which, as things were, prescribed contradictory courses of action. On the one hand, they commonly understood happiness as an individual state of mind, and, as Robert Mauzi has shown, prided themselves on being the first generation to examine the conditions necessary to it in a scientific manner. But on the other hand, they continually spoke of the 'happiness of the people', which, in the conditions of the eighteenth century, was connected with the idea of individual happiness only because it postulated the removal of certain obstacles to it. When the King of France in his edicts referred, as he customarily did, to 'le bonheur de mes peuples', all he meant was that it was his duty to mitigate as far as possible the worst disasters, such as plague, pestilence and famine, which to a greater or lesser extent afflicted every countryside in Europe, and that he should not bleed his subjects white by taxation. Before the rise in national incomes, however, that resulted from the industrial revolution, the achievement of even these objectives (as was proved in the Habsburg dominions during the reign of that enlightened despot Joseph II, and in France during the Revolution) was only capable of being realized, in so far as it could be realized at all, by a resort to violence and the arbitrary infringement of individual liberty and property rights totally incompatible with enlightened notions of individual happiness.

The same kind of contradictions, continually apparent but never acknowledged, characterized enlightened thinking on all the major social and political concepts with which the Philosophes concerned themselves. Liberty commonly meant to them the civil liberties, but it could mean other things as well. Montesquieu, for example, pointed out that 'it could happen that the constitution should be free and the citizen not free',[4] and then went on to say, in effect, that a man could only be considered free when he felt himself to be in control of his own destiny. Equality commonly meant equality before the law in the sense defined earlier, but frequently it also meant – as it did, for example, to Helvétius and Condorcet – if not equality of wealth at least a much closer approximation to it than existed anywhere in Europe at the time.

The Philosophes were united in their belief in happiness as the *summum bonum*, in reason as the instrument which governments should use to promote it, and in the rule of law and the civil liberties as necessary conditions of it. Except for these, in the existing conditions, to some extent contradictory general principles, however, they were agreed over nothing except their total condemnation of the existing order and the ideology on which it was based. Their first and most venomous attacks were directed against the Roman Catholic Church, which seemed to most of them the fountainhead of superstition and the most powerful obstacle in the way of a rational approach to the problems of life and government. But in their crusade against cruelty and oppression, and against misery in all its forms, which they saw as the result of ignorance and inefficiency and not of man's innate inhumanity to man, there was no social or political institution which escaped their condemnation, except that of absolutism itself. Though their denunciations of arbitrary power were in fact an indictment of it, to have condemned it openly would have been to preach revolution, which they never contemplated.

The doctrines of representative government and the sovereignty of the people owed their inspiration to contact with the Americans during the War of Independence, and to the shock administered to public confidence by the revelation of bankruptcy. Apart from Rousseau, whose *Contrat Social* made little impression at the time it was written, these doctrines found no champions before the eve of the Revolution, when they quickly became a divisive force. But the famous Philosophes, nearly all of whom were by this time dead, by continually denouncing the abuses of the régime, yet providing no programmes of reform which could provoke dissension, were able to cater for every kind of discontent, from that of the landless and starving to that of the principal beneficiaries of the régime, whose material advantages increasingly failed to compensate them for the arbitrariness and inefficiencies of absolutism.

The Enlightenment was the beginning of a new epoch in European thinking. The commonly held opinion, however, that it was a bourgeois movement, promoted by bourgeois in response to bourgeois needs, is far from wholly true. In social and political matters, it stood for values alien to the thinking of kings, churchmen and nobles in the days before the Philosophes had popularized their creed. In opposing the ideal of happiness (which, however understood, involved peace, tolerance and the absence of poverty and disease) to the military ideal; in opposing reason (that is, a critical examination of the means most appropriate to the promotion of happiness) to tradition and, as it was said, 'superstition' and 'fanaticism'; in opposing the rule of law and the civil liberties to privilege and paternalistic absolutism, the Enlightenment commanded the allegiance of the professional and business worlds in the nineteenth

80, 81 Rousseau and Voltaire (opposite), though they differed widely in their temperaments and opinions, agreed in their dislike of the old order. The satirical print (left) shows them in violent argument

century, though not of them alone, and served to promote their interests, which the old ideals had frustrated. In this sense, it may perhaps be described as a bourgeois movement. Its inspiration, too, was partly bourgeois. Its two most famous prophets, Voltaire and Diderot, were of bourgeois or plebeian origins; and Rousseau also, if one may reckon him among them. For though he repudiated the Philosophes' belief in reason as a means to progress, Rousseau shared, and was principally responsible for spreading, their view that men 'were not naturally wicked but only corrupted and miserable'.[5] With these admittedly notable exceptions, however, most of the famous prophets of the Enlightenment – Helvétius, for example, Holbach, Condorcet, Condillac, Mably – were born into the estate of the nobility, and it was in the aristocracy that it found its first and, until the eve of the Revolution, its most influential disciples.

82 Paul-Heinrich-Dietrich, Baron Holbach (1723–89), of German birth, one of the few avowed atheists among the Philosophes. He gave such generous hospitality to the circle of Encyclopaedists that he earned the title of *premier maître de l'hôtel de la philosophie*

The new ideas increasingly became the fashion among the educated and intelligent, particularly in the ruling class. Voltaire, in a letter to Helvétius in September 1763, wrote that the Philosophes had silenced their persecutors by ridicule, and the boast was justified. The Catholic Church, the privileged society, and absolutism in its existing form, found no defenders of any stature in the eighteenth century, apart from Montesquieu in his defence of privilege. The extent to which 'public opinion' (that is, the opinion in the *salons* where literary and political reputations were made and marred) moved to the side of the Philosophes was demonstrated by the reception which Voltaire received when the government allowed him to return from exile in 1778, and which Ségur, in a famous passage in his memoirs, described in the following words:

83  The crowning of Voltaire at the Théâtre Français, Paris 1778

The avenger of Calas, the apostle of liberty, the constant enemy and happy victor of prejudice and fanaticism, returned to Paris in triumph. The French Academy, whose precincts he hastened to visit, came out to welcome him, and after this public homage, which no prince had ever received, this prince of letters presided over the literary senate of France. Having returned to his house, transformed as it were into a palace by his presence, seated in the midst of a sort of council composed of Philosophes, and of the most daring and famous writers of the century, his courtiers were the most outstanding men of every class and the most distinguished foreigners of every nation.[6]

Thirteen years earlier, Horace Walpole, who had gone to Paris to cultivate the rich and the great and, as he said, 'went everywhere', and 'have been extremely visited', wrote to his friend, Seymour Conway: 'Do you know who the philosophers are or what the term means here? In the first place it comprehends almost everybody....'[7]

It was from the class of people with whom Horace Walpole associated, that is, the ruling class of *Les Grands*, that the ministers of the Ancien Régime were chosen. All of them (except Necker, who was a foreigner) were nobles. A number were people of remarkable intelligence; all had been subjected to the barrage of the new ideas; many, and particularly the holders of the post of Contrôleur Général, who had to deal with the key problems of the economy, found themselves in a position where reform seemed increasingly inescapable. Of the eighteen men who occupied this office, in effect if not in name, during the forty years before the Revolution, most were influenced by the enlightened ideas to some extent, and at least seven – Machault d'Arnouville, Silhouette, Bertin, Turgot, Necker, Calonne, and Brienne – are associated with attempts at reform that became increasingly radical. The proposals of the last three were, in fact, so sweeping that, had it been possible to put them into effect, they would have transformed the régime out of existence. The first serious converts of the Philosophes, and the men most deeply imbued with their ideas, were in fact the principal ministers and officials of the régime whose authority these ideas were in process of eroding.

Yet whatever the ultimate significance of the new ideology in destroying the foundations of belief on which absolutism and the privileged society rested, the explanation of the Ancien Régime's failure to transform itself without revolution must be sought in the impasse at which it had arrived by the end of the War of American Independence – an impasse of national bankruptcy arising from an economy overstrained by the exactions of half a century of war.

84 Jean Calas (1698–1762), Protestant merchant of Toulouse, was tortured and put to death by order of the Toulouse Parlement, allegedly for murdering his son to prevent his conversion to Catholicism. As a result of Voltaire's intervention Louis XV reversed this judgement and paid compensation to the Calas family, shown here

85, 86 Jacques Necker (1732–1804), born at Geneva and the successful head of a merchant bank in Paris, was in charge of the French finances from 1776 to 1781. The allegory on the right shows him being recalled to favour. He held office again from 1788 to 1789

## WAR AND NATIONAL BANKRUPTCY

By common consent, the crisis in France which led to the summoning of the States General, and so opened the way to the Revolution, was financial. By the summer of 1788 the government was bankrupt. The Contrôleur Général, Lambert, announced in August that the Treasury was empty and suspended all interest payments on the debt.

The immediate cause of this calamity, which had been imminent for some years, was the War of American Independence, into which France had entered in 1777 at a time when Necker was in control of

French financial affairs. Knowing that it was impossible to increase taxation, Necker had financed the war entirely out of loans. The French public at that time was so ignorant of the principles of government finance in general, and of the state of French finances in particular – always the most jealously guarded of government secrets – that Necker, as Mirabeau said, was acclaimed as a god because, unlike his predecessors, he had discovered a means of waging war that was painless to the tax-payer. The price that had to be paid for his miracle gradually came to light only after he fell from power in 1781.

The bankruptcy of 1788, however, was not merely the consequence of a single war. On the contrary, it was the more or less inevitable conclusion to half a century of financial mismanagement and failure to adapt an archaic system to changing needs. The French government, Marcel Marion pointed out in his *Histoire Financière de la France*, had never been solvent at any time since it had entered the War of the Austrian Succession in 1741. It had got through that war, and the Seven Years War of 1756–63, only by recurrently repudiating a part of its debts. After 1763 it was reduced to these practices, always described as partial bankruptcies, even in peace. The events of 1788 merely provided the final proof of that disparity between the objects of French policy and the means of attaining them that had distinguished the reign of Louis XIV and, under his successors, became increasingly obvious in the last forty years before the Revolution.

The principal functions of government in the eighteenth century, and the ones on which all the leading powers spent the bulk of their revenues, were the conduct of diplomacy and war. In France as in Britain, overwhelmingly the largest part of government expenditure went into the upkeep of the armed forces and paying the interest on the debt, itself the legacy of past wars. The accounts of the French government were always in such a state of confusion that no accurate figures are possible. One recent estimate, however, which is likely to be as good as any, puts the cost of these two items in 1786, a year of peace, at 74 per cent of total expenditure. The conclusion which this proportion suggests was drawn on various occasions by successive Contrôleurs Généraux in the years before the Revolution. When Calonne, for example, in 1787 summoned his Assembly of Notables (over a hundred eminent people selected from the most important corporations and other groups) to discuss remedies for the financial crisis, he pointed out that no significant economies were possible in the costs of internal administration or of the court. In any case, these amounted in conjunction to only about 26 per cent of the government's expenditure, which could only be drastically curtailed by cutting down on the major items, that is (and this was the course that proved inevitable), by bankruptcy and reductions in the armed forces.

In an age when governments were unable to mobilize resources for war directly by the control of production, trade and manpower, and could do so only indirectly by means of the purchasing power they acquired from taxes and loans, states measured their own and each other's war potential in terms of their power to tax and borrow – and ultimately in terms of their power to tax, since the interest on the debt could be paid only from the proceeds of the taxes. In these circumstances, wars came to an end not because physical resources of manpower and commodities were exhausted, but because it seemed impossible to raise from loans and taxes the sums that were necessary to keep armies in the field and ships at sea. The countries which first found themselves in this predicament lost the war, and this was the fate to which France succumbed in all the major wars, apart from the War of American Independence, that she waged in the hundred years before the Revolution.

It is commonly assumed that in the eighteenth century it was the defects in the French social and political arrangements that were responsible for this state of affairs. The argument could with equal cogency be put the other way round. Without the burdens which war imposed, the financial difficulties must have been less acute; the opportunities for waste would have been smaller; the taxes need not have been so heavy, and in that case the defects of the tax system, and the social, administrative and financial consequences of privilege, would have been less apparent. As Turgot said in 1776: 'When an imposition is very light the inequalities in its distribution may be an offence against exact justice but otherwise do no great harm. If two men have to carry a weight of 2 lbs between them, one could without inconvenience make the other carry the whole of it. If the weight were 200 lbs the man who carried it alone would have as much as he could carry and would suffer very impatiently that the other carried nothing. But if the weight were 400 lbs it would be absolutely necessary that it should be equally divided, since otherwise the man who carried it alone would succumb under it and it would not be carried.'[8]

Turgot compared the French peasants to the man who was required to carry 400 lbs. He believed that they were succumbing under their burdens and bringing the rest of the nation down with them. He hoped that this situation could be changed by reform, and it was indeed changed after the Revolution. Before then, however, the moral of his parable (and he himself drew it when he maintained that France could not afford to enter the War of American Independence) was that French foreign policy was too ambitious for a society that was unable to diminish privilege and administrative disorder.

French ambitions in the eighteenth century were the legacy of Louis XIV's triumphs. For nearly a quarter of a century after he had begun to rule, the French armies were unchallengeable. At his accession the Spaniards had reached the depths of their decline. The Dutch who, in their prime, had been a considerable military power, with the largest navy and merchant fleet in the world, had a population only one-tenth that of France. Their principal source of wealth, their commerce, was peculiarly vulnerable to attack. They were incapable of halting by themselves the French conquests, even though, after the French attacked them in 1672, they were able to free their own country of the invaders. The British, under Charles II and James II, were prevented from taking any active part in European affairs because of the disputes between Crown and Parliament. Among the remaining dynasties of Europe, including Britain's principal ally, the Habsburgs, there was none capable of a significant military effort unless financed by some other government. In these circumstances, as Bolingbroke once declared, the fear which France inspired among her potential victims was such that it 'not only hindered the growth of this power from being stopped in time, but nursed it up into a strength almost insuperable by any future confederacy'.[9]

It was the combined resources of Britain and the United Netherlands that changed this state of affairs. William III accepted the British Crown in order to enlist British resources in the war against Louis XIV, to whose defeat he dedicated his life. The British were willing to co-operate with him because they were equally menaced

87 Anne-Robert-Jacques Turgot, Baron de l'Aulne (1727–81), descended from an ancient noble family, *Intendant* of the Limousin (1761–74), Contrôleur Général (1774–6), friend of the Philosophes and the Physiocrats. He was the most famous of the reforming ministers and administrators of the Ancien Régime

by France. The French population outnumbered the British by about three to one. By 1672 Colbert had built up the French navy to a strength estimated as equivalent to that of the British and Dutch navies combined. After 1689 James II was an exile at the French court, and Louis was pledged to restore him to the British throne together, in the contemporary phrase, with 'popery and arbitrary power'. The treatment British Protestants might expect at French hands had been demonstrated by the Dutch experience between 1672 and 1674 and by the atrocities that had accompanied the revocation of the Edict of Nantes.

Inspired by Colbert, Louis XIV had, aimed at destroying the Dutch empire in the East Indies and ousting the United Netherlands, regardless of the fact that the French at that time lacked the technique to supplant them, from their position as the principal carriers of Europe's seaborne trade. At the end of his reign, he agreed to accept for his son the Spanish inheritance in Europe and the Western Hemisphere. Not only his power in Europe but his maritime and colonial ambitions were as much of a menace to the British as to the Dutch.

By 1689 the causes of conflict between Britain and France overseas, that dominated international relations in the eighteenth century, were already apparent. In the seventeenth and eighteenth centuries the areas of the world where white men could trade or settle were limited by difficulties of climate and transport, and by the attitudes of the indigenous populations. Where the nationals of one maritime European country managed to establish themselves, those of the other maritime countries attempted to follow; and immediately the representatives of the various European nations began to quarrel with each other over trade with the natives and over places of strategic importance for naval and commercial purposes. By the end of the seventeenth century, in most parts of the colonized world, the principal contestants for trade and territory were the British and the French.

In 1663 the French Crown took over the struggling French settlements in the valley of the St Lawrence, which had hitherto maintained an increasingly precarious existence under the aegis of a

88 Jean-Baptiste Colbert, Marquis de Seignelay (1619–83), principal minister of Louis XIV from 1661. Colbert was the son of a rich merchant who acquired a title and a *seigneurie*

Comme les Negres rament de bout

Commerce des Esclaves B.K.

89, 90 The slave trade was one of the most lucrative trades in the eighteenth century, in France as in England. Left, slave-trading in Martinique. Opposite, the Château de Serrant, built by one of the principal slave-traders in Nantes, an Irishman called Walsh, later created Comte de Serrant

chartered company, financed partly by the government and partly by private subscribers. Canada became 'New France' and Colbert pumped money and immigrants into it in the hope of founding a mighty empire in North America which should rival that of Spain and in which there should be no place for the British. The French and British settlers, living in close proximity in the St Lawrence valley, quarrelled with each other and their respective Indian allies, particularly over the fur trade. The founding of the British Hudson's Bay Company in 1670, which was able to tap sources of furs hitherto unexplored by the French, extended this quarrel to the north and west. In Newfoundland the British and the French disputed with each other over fishing rights. When La Salle discovered the source of the Mississippi, went down it to the Gulf of Mexico, and, in 1682, proclaimed the whole of the Mississippi basin, which he christened Louisiana, as belonging to the King of France, he conceived the idea, which the French were to put into operation some seventy years

later, of building a chain of forts in the valleys of the Mississippi and Ohio which would pen in the British settlers behind the Allegheny mountains.

In the West Indies, the British and French islands were sandwiched in amongst each other. Since the middle of the seventeenth century they had been valued by both nations principally because of the sugar they produced for sale in Europe. The production of the sugar, however, depended on a regular supply of slaves, over which the French and the British disputed in West Africa. The markets in the Spanish colonies, which the Spaniards themselves were unable to supply, and the positions of strategic importance which they occupied in the Caribbean, were a further and potent source of conflict between France and Britain, each of which was anxious to prevent the other from gaining control over the decaying Spanish Empire. Disputes comparable to those in the Western Hemisphere were to emerge in India in the middle of the eighteenth century.

147

All these causes of conflict sprang naturally out of conditions on the spot, and they gave rise to government policies which further exacerbated them. Both the French and British governments looked on colonies as a source of wealth to the mother country, which each desired to increase in its own case and to diminish in its rival's. Hence the laws governing colonial trade were devised as weapons of economic warfare, permitting, for example, the colonies within each empire to trade with each other and the mother country, but not with foreign countries or their dependencies, or in the ships belonging to them. As the British periodical, *The Craftsman*, founded in 1726, once put it: 'To utilize peace in order to procure ourselves the advantage of a large trade is to wage war on our enemies.'[10] Finally, colonial disputes over material interests, whether at a local or national level, were, to a greater or lesser extent in different parts of the world, inflamed by the religious and political passions that dominated relations between France and Britain in Europe in the time of Louis XIV. Particularly in North America, disputes over trade were accompanied by so many atrocities committed in the name of religion and national rivalry that each community grew to feel that it could not live in peace except by destroying the other.

The contest between France and Britain that began with William III's accession has been called 'the second hundred years war'. From the start, Britain was the senior partner in the Anglo-Dutch alliance. After William's death the power of the Dutch began to decline under the burden of the French wars. By the time of the Treaty of Utrecht, they had ceased to carry any weight in international affairs. In the eighteenth century they dissociated themselves from European problems more or less completely, and Britain was consequently left to carry on alone the tradition of opposing French expansion. Anglo-French hostility continued to dominate European politics, as the hostility between France, on the one hand, and Britain and Holland, on the other, had done earlier. Frederick the Great, in his memoirs, compared the French and the British in the eighteenth century to the leaders of two rival gangs who, 'the one by virtue of her armies and her great resources, the other by her fleets and the wealth she owed to her commerce',[11] tried to line up the kings and princes of Europe behind them. When France and Britain remained at peace, as they did notably from 1715 to 1740, no wars could assume significant proportions, since no other governments could provide the revenues necessary for prolonged fighting. When they decided to attack each other, war spread over the greater part of Europe, and over the seas, oceans and colonized areas of the world, until, for lack of money, the principal belligerents agreed to make peace, and forced their allies to do so also by withdrawing their subsidies.

In these respects, the pattern of events in Louis XIV's reign was repeated under his successors, but it changed increasingly in other ways. Though the population of France continued throughout the eighteenth century to exceed the British by about the same proportion as in Louis XIV's day, the British economy expanded faster than the French. It was even more significant that the British government could step up its expenditure in an emergency by a much higher proportion than could the French. The British government was compelled to render accounts of its expenditure to Parliament, which guaranteed to the holders of the debt the interest on their money. The financial position was kept continually under review. The honesty of the government in its relations with its creditors was beyond question. It was a principle with all British governments, which the immunity from invasion made it possible to observe, that the nation should have no more war than it could afford. These circumstances, which were without parallel in France, permitted British governments, through the mechanism provided by the Bank of England (to which there was also no equivalent in France because, among other reasons, the French government's honesty was always too suspect to permit it), to borrow much more easily in war and at a much lower rate of interest than the French. In consequence, though it would seem from such figures as are available that the British government's revenues in peace, even towards the end of the eighteenth century, cannot have been more than about half those of France, British expenditure, in the last stages of the two greatest wars of the century, seems likely to have exceeded that of the French.

Since the navy had first priority, British naval power, which had

91 The fortress of Louisbourg on the island of Cape Breton, which occupied over 100 acres, was the principal base for the trades between Canada, the French West Indies and metropolitan France, and for the French privateers who preyed on British shipping.

been much inferior to that of France in the time of Louis XIV, had increased by the middle of the eighteenth century to the point where the government could aim at always maintaining the Royal Navy at a strength equivalent to that of the navies of France and Spain combined. It achieved this objective, subject to the qualification that ships were laid up in peace and crews paid off, which meant that after the opening of hostilities it took time to get the navy on to a war footing.

British naval competition forced the French to put more of their resources into the war at sea, leaving them with fewer to deploy in Europe; and this happened at a time when states in central and eastern Europe – first the Prussians, then the Habsburgs, then the Russians – began to build up large standing armies. As a result of this combination of causes, the possibility of a French hegemony in Europe diminished until by 1748 it had altogether ceased to exist. The danger to Britain of French commercial competition, on the other hand, increased in the period that followed Louis XIV's wars. The second decade of the eighteenth century saw the beginning of a great expansion in French overseas trade and shipping. The French

92 Joseph-François, Marquis Dupleix (1697–1763), Clive's rival and model in the art of dominating India. The son of a General Farmer, Dupleix was the Governor General of the French settlements in India from 1742 to 1754

trades in tropical produce from the West Indies developed rapidly, together with the ancillary trade in slaves. French sugar outsold British on the markets of Europe. The French East India Company, which had been founded by Colbert but had perished during Louis XIV's wars, was reconstituted with the help of large government subsidies in the years after his death. The possibility of co-existence for Britain and France in India was suddenly brought to an end when the Governor-General of the French settlements there, Dupleix, acting on his own initiative, embarked on his attempts to conquer southern India in 1748. This action threatened to cut off the British from their Indian suppliers. The Directors of the British East India Company declared to the British government: 'If the French Court do support M. Dupleix's measures, or even if they do not disavow them, we apprehend it will be impossible for the East India Company to carry on their trade.'[12] At the same time, in North America, the French began to construct the chain of forts in the valleys of the Mississippi and Ohio which La Salle had regarded earlier as the essential means of preventing the westward expansion of the British colonists. As they observed all these developments, the British government concluded that the French were bent on destroying their colonies and ruining their commerce. The French, meanwhile, with equal justice and more cause for fear, made the same assumptions about the British.

The British owed the increasing success of their naval wars with France in the first three-quarters of the eighteenth century to more rational policies and a better allocation of resources, combined with a virtual immunity from invasion. The British government, relying on the protection afforded by the English Channel, could economize on armaments in peace, and build them up gradually after the outbreak of war. It disposed of its resources according to policies that were evolved gradually, that were applied more or less successfully at different times (achieving complete success only during Chatham's great ministry), but that, before the War of American Independence, always permitted it ultimately to achieve supremacy at sea. The French government, in this as in other matters, was unable to pursue a consistent policy, and dissipated its resources between the war at sea and on the Continent, thus achieving victory in neither.

To Britain, trade, and colonies as a means to trade, and sea-power as a means of protecting both, seemed the prerequisites of British prosperity and the highest concern of government policy. The control of events in Europe appeared subsidiary to these ends. To the French, on the other hand, it was the control of events in Europe that was of primary concern. Trade and colonies, and the sea-power to protect them, seemed necessary only because, as long as Colbert's views prevailed, they were judged, as in England, to be the principal source of wealth from which wars were financed.

To the British, control of events in Europe always appeared essential in the eighteenth century for two reasons. In the first place they could not tolerate that any power should dominate the Continent. They had resisted Louis XIV's attempts to do this, and they resisted those of Louis XV when, in 1741, he seized the occasion of Prussia's attack on Silesia to organize a league against the Habsburgs. His object was to parcel out the Habsburg dominions among his satellites (in which category he included Prussia), and to bestow the imperial dignity on his puppet, Charles Albert of Bavaria. The British felt obliged to resist these ambitions for many reasons, but principally because a power that dominated the Continent could also dominate the seas, and hence the colonized areas of the world, which were dependent on sea-power for their defence. If the French encountered no obstacles in Europe to the pursuit of their policies, then they could deprive Britain of her Continental markets, shut her out from her vital sources of naval stores in the Baltic (without which she could not build or equip her navies), force the smaller sea-faring states to put their ships at France's disposal and, in general, gain access to resources that would enable France to construct a navy superior to the Royal Navy.

In the second place, even when the French were not in a position to dominate the Continent – and they were forced to abandon this attempt after 1748 – the British could not dissociate themselves from European affairs. They needed European allies because, with their smaller population and national income, they could not stand up alone to France. One of the prerequisites of British victory in any war with France was the existence of states on the Continent to whose interest it was to fight the French and who, helped by British subsidies, would put armies into the field that would deflect French resources from the war at sea.

It was to France's interest to prevent such a state of affairs from developing. This was, however, an interest which the French could not pursue except by abandoning their claims, if not to dominate, at least to exercise a determining voice in Europe. Though in the hundred years before the Revolution there was no power on the Continent that menaced France's security, her traditions had been moulded in times when invasion was a real danger. The large and, for the greater part, poverty-stricken French nobility continued, as in Louis XIV's reign, to see war, in the words of Francis Parkman, 'as its only worthy calling and prized honour more than life'.[13] The great achievements of Louis XIV in his early days set the standard for future generations. These traditions were too strong for the last two Bourbons before the Revolution, who were both unwarlike by temperament. Louis XV had been pushed into the War of the

Austrian Succession against his better judgement and that of his chief minister, Cardinal Fleury, by the machinations of a clique at Court. Its leader, the Comte (later Maréchal and Duc) de Belleisle, pointed out that Louis would be unworthy of his ancestors if he failed to seize the opportunity which then presented itself to revenge the defeats of Louis XIV's latter years and to establish a French hegemony in Europe. Even when, after 1748, hegemony was no longer possible, and tension was mounting in the colonies, Louis, with an ineptitude that was a by-word in French history until the subject palled, allowed himself to be inveigled into an alliance with the Habsburgs, whose purpose was to regain Silesia and dismember the Hohenzollern dominions, and whose actions set the stage for the

93, 94 Right, Nicolas Fouquet, Comte de Melun et de Vaux, Marquis de Belleisle, descended from an ancient family of soldiers and magistrates, *Surintendant des Finances* from 1653 to 1662. Left, his château of Vaux-le-Vicomte

Seven Years War – the last of the great world wars before the Revolution.

The pattern of military events which brought about the French defeat between 1759 and 1763 was similar to that which had emerged at the end of the War of the Austrian Succession. Then, however, it had been created accidentally, whereas in the Seven Years War it was the result of deliberate calculation. The military genius of Chatham, and the unprecedented degree of control (by eighteenth-century standards) he was able to exercise over his colleagues, so that all naval and military operations could be planned as the component parts of a grand strategy, brought victory more quickly and on a larger scale than on any previous occasion.

155

95 This engraving of the Battle of the Plains of Abraham, 1759, an early example of com-

British government expenditure at the beginning of the war had been between £6 and £7 millions. It had risen to over £21 millions by 1761, when for two years Choiseul had been telling his Austrian allies that France was bankrupt. It enabled the British government to build and repair ships in much larger numbers than the French. In this and other ways it provided the physical prerequisites of a powerful navy which were absent in France and which must go a long way to explain those defects in French naval strategy on which naval historians always insist. And having, by superior strength, destroyed the French navy, the British had at their mercy not only the trade and colonies of France, but also those of Spain, who joined France in 1762. Canada was conquered in 1759. In that year and the years that followed, the French slaving-stations in West

bined operations, telescopes the battle into one scene. Quebec lies in the background

Africa and virtually all the French West Indian islands were captured and French power in India destroyed. Havana, the great convoy assembly-point and centre of the Spanish imperial trades, on which the revenues of the Spanish Crown largely depended, surrendered to the British in August 1762. At the same time, every neutral seafaring nation found its ships at the mercy of the Royal Navy, which claimed the right to search them for blockade-running, in accordance with rules of the British government's devising, and, for the sake of the prize-money, frequently seized them and their cargoes even when they had observed the rules. Not surprisingly in these circumstances, the cry went up all over Europe that Louis XIV's power and arrogance paled into insignificance by comparison with those of this new mistress of the seas.

96 Etienne-François, Duc de Choiseul (1719–85), soldier, diplomat and statesman, Minister of Foreign Affairs and Louis XV's principal adviser from 1758 to 1770

To the ruling class in France this reversal of fortunes seemed an insupportable humiliation. Apart from Canada, which had always been an economic liability to the French government, the British in 1763 gave back to the French most of the territories they had conquered from them. It was not, however, material interests that were primarily at stake in France. As Vergennes, who became foreign minister after Louis XVI's accession, put it in a draft memorandum for the King: 'The humiliating peace of 1763 . . . has given rise to the opinion in every nation that France has no longer any strength or resources. . . . It is enough to read the Treaty of Paris, and particularly the negotiations which preceded it, to realize the ascendancy which England has acquired over France and to judge how much that arrogant nation savours the pleasure of having humiliated us.' The humiliation was unjust, Vergennes concluded (though largely in defiance of the facts), because 'its principle and object was the pride of a powerful rival'. France, he deduced in consequence, was obliged 'for the sake of her honour, her dignity and her reputation' to take her revenge as soon as the opportunity presented itself.[14] It did so when the American colonies revolted.

The problem which had always faced the French government was how to dominate, or exercise a preponderant influence, on the Continent without provoking Britain to frustrate this object by the dual policy of supporting France's enemies in Europe and destroying her overseas trade, so that bankruptcies spread throughout the shipping and trading communities and undermined the credit on which the government depended to finance its war effort. The answer which occurred later to the Jacobins and to Napoleon, and which Marshal Saxe appears, in effect, to have recognized at the end of the War of the Austrian Succession, was that Europe should be conquered and its resources afterwards mobilized to defeat the mistress of the seas in her own element. In the days of Louis XV and Louis XVI, however, this was too unconventional and hazardous a project to be considered. The alternative solution was to refrain from provoking or abetting disputes in Europe and to concentrate on the war at sea. This was the solution which occurred to Choiseul as a result of his experiences in the Seven Years War, and which he

97 Charles-Gravier, Comte de Vergennes (1717–87), member of a provincial Robe family, pupil of Choiseul and his successor as Foreign Minister

98, 99 An example of French naval architecture which was superior to the British in the eighteenth century, notwithstanding the much more successful record of Britain in sea

educated his successor, Vergennes, to adopt. When France entered the War of American Independence, she preserved the peace in Europe, and as a result Britain was defeated.

The British defeat, however, came too late. After the war was over, the imminence of bankruptcy forced the French to withdraw from European affairs altogether. Even the purpose of the war – the crippling of British trade – was not attained, for British trade with the Western Hemisphere, so far from diminishing, increased after the American colonies had been lost.

To those looking for the causes of the collapse of the Ancien Régime one of the principal ones may thus be said to lie in Anglo-French relations. Of the hundred years that elapsed between 1689 and the Revolution, nearly half were spent in wars with Britain. They involved the French government in continually mounting costs. They overburdened the economy and reduced the system of

warfare. Above, cutaway view of a French two-decker, showing life aboard a warship. Below, French naval architects at work

taxation to chaos. They were one of the main obstacles in the way of reform, because most of the projected reforms would have involved a temporary loss of revenue, and this could never be afforded. The recurrent partial bankruptcies and the continual attempts to increase taxation were among the most potent causes of discontent. The military failures of the first two wars of the eighteenth century brought the government into contempt. The successes in the last war, which was fought to win the Americans their freedom, undermined the old ideals of absolutism and privilege and promoted the new ideas of liberty and equality for which the Americans stood.

The principal problems which faced the French government in the second half of the eighteenth century were the ones which had faced its predecessors time out of mind: how to raise enough money from taxation at any given moment to meet the government's immediate needs, and how to increase the resources of the tax-payers in the long run so that they should have more to give. In the second half of the eighteenth century, however, these problems were approached in a new spirit. Louis XIV had followed the traditions of his ancestors in his pursuit of glory. He had followed their methods, too, by embarking on his grandiose projects without counting the cost, and by raising the money to pay for them by whatever means were at hand, regardless of the social, financial and economic consequences. He had financed his wars on the principle that expenditure need never be related to revenue and that 'extraordinary financial operations' would always enable 'the government to net in as much as it wished to spend'.[1] The result, by 1715, had been the ruin of agriculture and of most trades and industries, a general bankruptcy, and profit only for the *traitants*, or financiers in the Crown's service. The Regency, after Louis' death, attempted to sacrifice the *traitants* to the public's demand for vengeance and to its own need for money, by bringing them before a so-called 'chambre de justice', which sought to mulct them of their fortunes. The more substantial among them, however, all succeeded in bribing their way out.

Increasingly, throughout the second half of the eighteenth century, and in spite of continuing admiration for many of the achievements of Louis XIV's reign, all the items in this sequence of events came to be looked on with horror because in their results they were arbitrary, unjust, inhumane and economically disastrous. The gulf that separated the end of the seventeenth century from the end of the eighteenth is typified by the words of Calonne in a letter he wrote to Louis XVI in 1787, after he had been dismissed from the post of Contrôleur Général: 'May one banish for ever the false and murderous idea that the state can be helped by bankruptcy. You have always known me, Sire, to reject it with horror. Of whatever kind it might be, partial or complete, direct or indirect, and by whatever name one might disguise it, it would always be not only unjust, barbarous and dishonourable, but ruinous rather than beneficial to the financial situation.'[2] How to avert it had been the major problem since the great wars of the eighteenth century had started. The more urgent the problem grew, however, the wider the tasks involved in solving it appeared, until they seemed to require the recasting of every major social and political institution.

The first reformers, imbued with the authoritarian traditions of the French monarchy and an enlightened dislike of privilege, concentrated on reducing the tax privileges of the nobility. Machault d'Arnouville, Contrôleur Général from 1745 to 1754, a man of strong character but narrow vision, commonly described as cold, haughty and taciturn, subjected noble landowners in 1749 for the first time to a permanent direct tax, the *vingtième*, equivalent to the English land-tax at 1s. in the £. Later the *vingtième* was doubled and then tripled and further augmented by various supplements and other taxes. Since the landlord's tenants, who were not noble, had always been subject to the *Taille*, and, as was undisputed knowledge at the time, passed it on to him to a greater or lesser extent, the French government by these measures plainly attempted to subject its nobility to a much heavier rate of direct taxation than fell on the equivalent classes in England. In England the land-tax was never even nominally more than 4s. in the £ and in practice was always much less; and on land that was leased out, it was paid by the tenant, who deducted it from his rent.

Machault d'Arnouville's ambitions were doomed to failure. The bulk of the nobility, much poorer than their English counterparts, found it difficult to make ends meet. They themselves, and the *Intendants* and provincial Parlements speaking on their behalf, continually complained that the taxes threatened them with ruin. There is proof that these complaints were sometimes justified; and

100 Jean Baptiste de Machault, Seigneur D'Arnouville (1701–94), descended from a distinguished Robe family, Contrôleur Général (1745–54) Keeper of the Seals (1750–5), Secretary of State for the Navy (1754–7), author of the first permanent direct tax on the nobility

they may have been so to a greater extent than the available evidence suggests, since it was to the Crown's interest to collect evidence in the contrary sense.

The government continually complained that the nobles evaded their taxes. Indeed it seems clear that Machault d'Arnouville and his successors induced in noble minds the sense of injustice and the mutinous determination not to pay, which had long been characteristic of the peasantry. This was a state of affairs with which the administration was unable to cope. The tax-collectors were, for the greater part, uneducated and open to bribery and intimidation. Either the pressures to which they were subjected, or the temptation to pay off old scores to which they were accused of succumbing, or defects in the law itself, produced extraordinary anomalies even in the treatment received by neighbours in closely comparable circumstances. Among the twenty richest landowners in Toulouse, for example, there was one in 1750 (that is, at a date when taxation was

165

much lower than it was to become later) who paid in direct taxes 31 per cent of a gross landed income equivalent to about £280 in the English currency of the time. There was another who, on a rather larger income, paid only 8 per cent.

The attempts to tax the nobility produced much injustice and ill-feeling, and yet yielded results that were financially negligible. Principally, however, this happened, not because of tax-evasion or defects in the methods of assessment, but because the nobles accounted for only between 1 and 2 per cent of the population, and most of them were poor. Very few of them possessed the large fortunes which, whether it was social justice or the royal revenues that were at issue, were the obvious targets for attack, but targets, nevertheless, which could not be reached by any methods known to eighteenth-century administrations.

Various circumstances in French life in the eighteenth century combined to focus attention on the small number of the very rich to a degree not paralleled in England, though conditions there were not incomparable. The growing poverty in the countryside and the growing luxury in the towns; the Crown's financial difficulties, combined with the pensions it gave to courtiers and other members of the ruling class (although these were in fact an insignificant item in total government expenditure); the great wealth of the tax-farmers, which, though not in the ordinary sense of the term dis-honestly come by, was nevertheless derived from the oppression of the people – all these things increasingly made the large fortunes seem a crying scandal to enlightened French minds. But the large fortunes were an integral part of the social and political system which it was beyond the power of the reformers to touch. All governments in the eighteenth century were forced to tolerate great inequalities of wealth. All governments, the British included, were impotent to impose direct taxes on incomes derived from commerce, industry or finance. No government possessed the techniques necessary to tax directly any source of income except land. No government could tax the land except at a flat rate which was calculated to drive the poorer landowners bankrupt (supposing they could be made to pay) before it significantly affected the rich.

In attempting to subject the nobles to increasingly heavier taxation the French government merely exasperated them and increased the tensions within the order, without benefit to itself. It could hardly have done otherwise so long as the volume of taxation could not be reduced, and fell more heavily on the bulk of the peasantry than on any other group. Increasingly, however, the realization grew that the solution to the Crown's difficulties lay not so much in attempts at distributing more equally a burden that, given the defects of the administration, was too heavy in any case, but in an overhaul of the whole financial system, and in an increase in productivity, the need for which came to obsess the French reformers more than it can have obsessed any ministers before the twentieth century.

The way the enlightened ministers finally came to see things was expressed by Calonne in the speech he made to the Assembly of Notables, summoned to consider the financial crisis in the spring of 1787. Having described the government's desperate financial position, and shown that there were no possible economies that could serve to fill 'this frightful void', he asked 'what remains that can possibly supply all that is wanted and procure that which the restoration of the finances requires?' He gave the following answer:

It is in the correction of abuses that a fund of riches is to be found, which the state has a right to appropriate, and which should be converted to the purpose of restoring order. It is there that the only means of supplying all the exigencies are to be found. It is from the very bosom of disorder that must issue the fruitful source which will fertilize every part of the monarchy. . . . The abuses which the business of this day goes to annihilate for the public good, are the most considerable, the most protected, and such as have the deepest root, and the most luxuriant branches. These are the abuses, the existence of which weighs heaviest upon the useful and laborious classes; the abuses of pecuniary privileges; the exceptions to the common law, and so many unjust exemptions, which relieve one part of those who should contribute, and aggravate the burthens of the other; the general inequality in apportioning the subsidies and the enormous disproportion which exists in the contributions of the different provinces . . . the rigour and arbitrary construction in levying the Taille; the fear, the constraint, and the something like dishonour, under which the commerce in the produce of the earth labours: the custom-houses for levying the internal duties of entry and those barriers which render the different parts of the Kingdom strangers to each other: the duties which discourage industries, those which are excessively expensive in the collecting and require a vast number of officers, those which have a tendency to encourage smuggling, and which, every year, are the destruction of thousands of citizens. . . . In short, all that discourages the produce, all that enfeebles the resources of credit, all that renders the revenue unproductive and all the superfluous expenses which absorb it.[3]

101, 102 In the caricature below satirizing the *Assemblée des notables* which Calonne convoked in 1787 to review the financial situation, the president (monkey) asks the notables (geese) with what sauce they would like to be eaten. Opposite, the *Assemblée des notables* presided over by Louis XVI

It was indeed true that a principal cause of the abuses lay, as Calonne said, in 'the very bosom of disorder', that is, in the central administration of financial affairs. The government had always lived from hand to mouth. There was no department in control of public spending, and before the very eve of the Revolution nothing that corresponded to a budget. The treasury was only one of many agencies that received and disbursed the tax-payers' money, and it has been estimated that in 1788 it was responsible for only half of this. Though the various government departments were required to keep accounts, all kept them on different principles so that they could never be amalgamated, and all were many years in arrears. It was never possible to estimate how much had been spent in any previous year or would be available in any present or future one. Thus no order of priorities could be established and consequently no restraint put on wasteful or imprudent expenditure.

From this situation arose the 'fiscalism' – that is, the practice of running the administration with the primary object of obtaining money for immediate needs – that was largely responsible for the unproductive revenues to which Calonne referred. The direct taxes were levied by an army of royal tax-collectors to whom the Crown had sold their offices in numbers dictated by financial rather than administrative needs; over whom, since it could not afford to buy them out, it could exercise only an inadequate control; and who were entitled to retain for themselves a proportion of the receipts on which it was impossible to keep an adequate check. The indirect taxes were levied by the tax-farm, which, as the eighteenth century progressed, became increasingly more efficient as a revenue-raising organization, but whose purpose was to produce the largest possible revenue regardless of the effects on trade and industry. In deference to this principle, and also to provincial liberties, internal trade was subject to an enormous number of tolls and customs barriers, which the General Farmers maintained their army of tax-inspectors to enforce. 'Trade', it has been said, 'suffered not only from the taxes that were rising and becoming more difficult to evade, but also from the more exacting administration of a system of unfathomable complexity.'[4] After 1786, when the British and the French, by the

103 Charles-Alexandre de Calonne, Comte d'Hannonville (1734–1802), the descendant of a provincial Robe family ennobled in the seventeenth century, *Intendant* of Metz and then of Lille (1766–83), Contrôleur Général from 1783 to 1787

Eden Treaty, agreed to lower the tariff barriers between them, it emerged that the duty imposed on British goods entering the country was no higher than the duty which French manufacturers (already subject to duties on their raw materials) paid on their finished products in transit between one part of France and another.

The object of the enlightened ministers was to free enterprise from the shackles which were placed on it, in these and other ways, by a régime whose professions of paternalistic benevolence cloaked a state of affairs that one Englishman, who was required in 1831 to report to the House of Commons on French financial arrangements, and who pushed his investigations back into the Ancien Régime, described as 'rapine unbounded, confusion inextricable, delay interminable, vexations infinite; the whole machinery seemingly so contrived that the greatest burdens to the subject should produce the smallest benefit to the State'.[5]

As an intelligent pupil of the Enlightenment, Calonne, like Turgot and Necker before and Brienne after him, stressed administrative disorder as a principal cause of France's failure to expand economically to the extent which was necessary and which seemed to him possible. In the same spirit he also stressed 'the ancient prejudices which antiquity seems to have given a sanction to'; by which he meant 'l'empire de l'habitude'[6] – the dominance of custom – to quote the words of one enlightened *Intendant*. These two causes of economic backwardness acted and reacted on each other. In a piecemeal fashion, and to the limits of their power, Calonne's predecessors, in the thirty years before the Revolution, had attempted to attack both. The disease had by this time, however, reached a point at which it defied the application of piecemeal remedies and limited power.

The enlightened ministers found the dominance of custom most sinister in the countryside. From the end of the Seven Years War, the peasants had seemed to them to pose the problem on whose solution the future of France depended, since they constituted the overwhelming majority of the population, and a poor peasantry meant a poor nation and a poor government. The example of England pointed the way to what could be done. *Vaine pâture* became, in Marc Bloch's words, 'the subject of a veritable anathema'.

104 Cardinal Etienne-Charles Loménie de Brienne (1724–94), the son of an impoverished noble family whose fortunes he hoped to rehabilitate by entering the Church, Bishop of Toulouse in 1763. In 1787 he succeeded Calonne as Contrôleur Général with the title of head of the Council of Finance

One of the magistrates of the Parlement of Metz once said: 'we might perhaps not have realized that this practice was a bad one if the English had not taught us what the land is capable of. Without the shadow cast by the picture of their agriculture on ours, we might still believe like our fathers that the rights of *vaine pâture* were not a bondage.'[7]

Most people in all walks of life nevertheless continued to believe as their fathers had believed. The government set up ministerial committees on agriculture. It encouraged the founding of agricultural societies all over France. It supplemented these measures by edicts permitting landowners in a number of provinces to enclose the whole or part of their property. It failed, however, to elicit a significant response.

Only the richer landowners had consolidated their holdings in the open fields and could afford the cost of enclosing them. But if they attempted to do this, they ran the risk of having their fences pulled down by the villagers and their actions declared illegal by either the *Intendant* or the provincial Parlement. Admittedly these authorities were commonly at loggerheads. On the question of *vaine pâture*, however, both were apt to take the side of the poor, the *Intendants* principally because of their fear of riots and of a fall in the taxes, the Parlements for the reason that a high official of the Paris Parlement, Joly de Fleury, gave in 1766 when he was consulted on the matter. 'The rights of *vaine pâture*', he said, 'having been established for the greater part by customary arrangements, it does not seem possible to interfere with them since they constitute a sort of property belonging to the community of inhabitants.'[8]

105 Guillaume-François Joly de Fleury (1710–87), descended from one of the most influential Robe dynasties whose members had been magistrates and administrators since the beginning of the sixteenth century

106 Henri-Léonard-Jean-Baptiste Bertin, Comte de Bourdeilles (1719–92), descended from a noble Robe family. A noted agronomist, he was *Intendant* of Roussillon, then of Lyon, and Contrôleur Général (1759–63)

The enlightened ministers could see no way out of these difficulties. Though a modernized agriculture, as the Physiocrats continually emphasized, would ultimately have benefited everyone, the problem was how to effect the changeover. Were the many peasants who owned little or no land, and supplemented their meagre resources by the animal or two they pastured on the common fields, to be driven by force to the destitution with which enclosure seemed to threaten them? As Bertin said: 'It is between the protection that is due to the suffering part of humanity and the greater benefit to agriculture as a whole, that it is difficult to decide.'[9] Were the more substantial land-holding peasants, whose strips lay scattered over the open fields, to be forced to consolidate them? For nothing short of force could have brought this result about, so attached were the peasant proprietors to their particular plots of land and so convinced that any arrangement desired by their superiors could only be to their disadvantage. Coercion, however, seemed unthinkable to the enlightened ministers

175

who, though hostile to privilege and prepared, if driven to it, to coerce the better-to-do up to a point, always made an exception for the basic rights, such as they were, of the peasants. As Calonne said: 'the greatest of all abuses would be to begin with those . . . existing only among the poor'.

Thus the reforming ministers never gave to landowners a general or unqualified permission to enclose. Marc Bloch provides a great deal of evidence, however, to show that no class of landowners in fact desired this. Apart from a few exceptional cases, rich and poor alike showed no interest in the new agriculture. The richer land-owners often acquired permission to enclose their meadows and to take in land from the waste. They were happy, however, to continue with the communal cultivation of the arable land which they found many ways of exploiting, as it seemed, to their own benefit. The attempt to inaugurate an agricultural revolution thus came to grief. 'The impression of all the observers in the generation which saw the application of the reforms', Marc Bloch writes, 'was that of a great set-back.'[10]

By failing to have an agricultural revolution, Lefebvre once observed, the French condemned themselves to the social and political revolution they experienced in and after 1789. This could not be disputed, but is true only because of the other conditions which existed in France in the second half of the eighteenth century. There is no reason to suppose that the misery and desperation of the French peasants were any greater than those of the followers of Pugachev in Russia, or of the Bohemian peasants who rose in revolt during the famine of 1771. Indeed, there is good reason to suppose they were less, since the Russian and Bohemian peasants rose against governments that were firmly in control and could suppress them without much difficulty. Their actions were, in a literal sense, desperate. The French peasants, on the other hand, who burned the châteaux and the manorial records in the spring and summer of 1789, made no move until law and order had already begun to collapse as a result of the resistance provoked by the government's attempts at reform. They seized the opportunity presented to them by the weakness of a government in its death agonies.

The people who led the third estate (that is, in this connection, certain sections of the bourgeoisie) against the privileged orders did the same. When, in February 1789, Calonne, then in exile in London, wrote to Louis XVI to outline the reforms he thought necessary, he said in one place: 'when I began this letter I was unaware of the extent to which a division had developed between the nobility and the third estate in various provinces of your kingdom. Since I have heard of it I tremble.'[11] A large body of evidence could be produced to support his testimony to the suddenness with which this division manifested itself.

Until the end of the 1780s, the struggle for reform had never been between the third estate (or any section of it) and the nobility, though as the Revolutionary propaganda took shape this is what was said and what later generations came to believe. The antagonists, it was maintained, were the privileged classes on the one hand, and the unprivileged – the third estate – on the other. This proposition had only to be formulated to acquire substance, for the nobility drew together as they were attacked. In fact, however, the three orders or estates into which pre-revolutionary French society was divided by law had never constituted social classes. Each estate contained within itself a variety of such classes, commonly in conflict with one another though capable of combining against a common enemy. Privileged groups in large numbers existed within each of the three estates, but also transcended them, as in the national corporations or analogous bodies – for example, the Church, the Parlements and the tax-farm, where nobles and *roturiers* formed part of an organization which, most conspicuously in the case of the Parlements, inspired in its members a corporate loyalty.

In these circumstances the only initiators of practical reforms could have been, and were, the enlightened ministers and their staffs, during such periods as they enjoyed the king's support. Their opponents, as is illustrated in particular by the failure to reform agriculture and to abolish the internal customs barriers and the guilds (the counterparts in the spheres of trade and industry to the *servitudes collectives* on the land), were the corporate bodies whose rights the projected reforms menaced. As one intelligent observer, Rabaut

177

107 Marie-Antoinette
in rustic costume
◀ (*en Gaulle*),
by Elisabeth Vigée-Lebrun,
1783

108 Louis XVI
by J. S. Duplessis,
*c.* 1780

Saint-Étienne, put it: 'every time one creates a corporate body with privileges one creates a public enemy because a special interest is nothing else than this. . . . Imagine a country where there are a great many corporate bodies. The result is that . . . one hears talk of nothing but rights, concessions, immunities, special agreements, privileges, prerogatives. Every town, every community, every province, every ecclesiastical or judicial body, has its interest to defend in this confusion. . . . A minister who wants to disentangle the wires does not know where to begin because as he touches them he makes the interest cry out to which they are attached.'[12]

The reforming ministers did, indeed, find themselves in the position which Rabaut Saint-Étienne described. As soon as their projects aroused opposition, cliques formed against them in the *salons* and the Court, and prevailed on the king to dismiss them. As they touched the wires which made the vested interests cry out, these found support in the powerful corporations, and particularly in the Parlements, whose leading members were prominent in high society. Though most of the reforming ministers began their careers in the Parlements, which provided the Enlightenment with many distinguished apostles, in their collective capacity these corporations were the most redoubtable defenders of the existing order. Every project for reform was liable ultimately to come up against their opposition and to founder on their refusal to register the royal edicts. While, however, the Parlements defended the tax privileges of the nobility, the monopolies of the guilds, the rights of the village communities in the matter of *vaine pâture*, and indeed every other kind of privilege, they increasingly attacked the absolute

109, 110, 111, 112 Establishment renegades. Far left, Marie-Jean, Hérault de Séchelles, a rich epicurean who became President of the Convention under the Terror. Left, Antoine-Joseph-Michel Servan, *avocat général* at the Grenoble Parlement from 1764, and author of a number of revolutionary pamphlets. Right, Louis-Michel Le Peletier de St Fargeau, a radical, who was Président of the Paris Parlement in 1789 and went over to the patriots on the Revolution. Overleaf, Philippe Egalité (Louis-Philippe-Joseph d'Orléans, Duc de Chantilly), cousin of Louis XVI, who joined the revolutionary party from the outset

power of the monarch, whose authority they attempted to circumscribe by actions strongly reminiscent of those of the English Parliaments under the Stuarts. They justified this behaviour in terms of precedent, but in fact precedent supported them even less than it had supported their English predecessors. In their denunciations of arbitrary power, and of the infringement of individual liberties which occurred when the government, driven to distraction by their obstructiveness, took action against them, the Parlements spoke not in the language appropriate to absolutism, but in the language of the Enlightenment. Down to the eve of the Revolution, as has often been pointed out, their continual defiance of the royal authority, and their remonstrances, which were printed and widely circulated, were more responsible for inflaming opinion against the government than any other single cause.

This state of affairs was also typical. The prophets of the Enlightenment had continually inveighed against privilege – both in the old sense of particular rights guaranteed by law to particular groups, and

113 Monsieur Lucas at the Palais Royal: caricature of 1789 showing a ridiculous country deputy arriving for the Third Estates with a tree of liberty in his hand and welcomed by the ladies

in the new sense of wealth unjustified by service to the community. But they had also continually inveighed against arbitrary power. While they had provided the reformers with their inspiration, and fostered a general mood of revolt, they had put a weapon into the hands of every group whose rights were attacked. For privilege, however understood, could not be reduced to manageable proportions, let alone abolished, except by action that was arbitrary, not only by enlightened standards, but even by the standards of absolutism.

In his *Introduction à la Révolution Française*, Barnave said that, by the time of Louis XVI's accession, the Crown had reached the point when it had only two choices: it must turn itself into either a military despotism or a constitutional monarchy. In fact, neither of these alternatives was practicable at any period in the history of the Ancien Régime. On the one hand, to abolish ancient institutions and

183

rights by force was wholly alien to the ideas and practices of Western absolutism; on the other hand, government by consent was equally alien to them and impracticable for another reason. As the Philosophes always knew – though the matter was one they generally chose not to discuss, but preferred to shelve, as did Rousseau and many others, by involking that *deus ex machina*, the 'legislator' – the tasks that needed to be accomplished were not ones for which any measure of consent could have been found.

Denied by absolutism the machinery and the chance to develop the habits of mind necessary for political discussion, without parties or programmes, atomized by privilege, as Tocqueville pointed out, into an almost infinite number of mutually hostile groups which could only be prevented from flying at each other's throats by compromises which solved no problems, French society in the second half of the eighteenth century was incapable of reforming itself by peaceful means. It was equally incapable of being reformed from above, except on the improbable assumption that a man with the qualities of a Napoleon should have inherited the French throne, and should have survived the upbringing to which, in such circumstances, he would have been subjected.

114 Allegory on the Revolution picturing Rousseau as its spiritual father, presiding over a number of symbols.
These include a monument to Equality, two maidens representing Goodness and Good Faith, a bundle of rods and war axes (efficient administration and the enforcement of laws) ▶
topped by the red Cap of Liberty;
the Eye of Providence emitting the light of Wisdom, a Tree of Liberty, unfinished columns (the bases of regeneration),
a soldier of the Revolution, and, in the dim background, a guillotine

KINGDOM OF SWEDEN

Baltic Sea

DUCHY OF COURLAND

Düna

DOMINIONS OF HOHENZOLLERNS

Vistula

Oder

KINGDOM OF POLAND

Dniester

DOMINIONS OF THE HABSBURGS

Danube

REPUBLIC

Adriatic Sea

REP. OF RAGUSA

Sea

KINGDOM OF THE TWO SICILIES

Sea

RUSSIAN EMPIRE

Oka

Volga

Don

Dnieper

Sea of Azov

Black Sea

OTTOMAN EMPIRE

Aegean Sea

115 Europe about 1786, showing the lands of the five major military powers

187

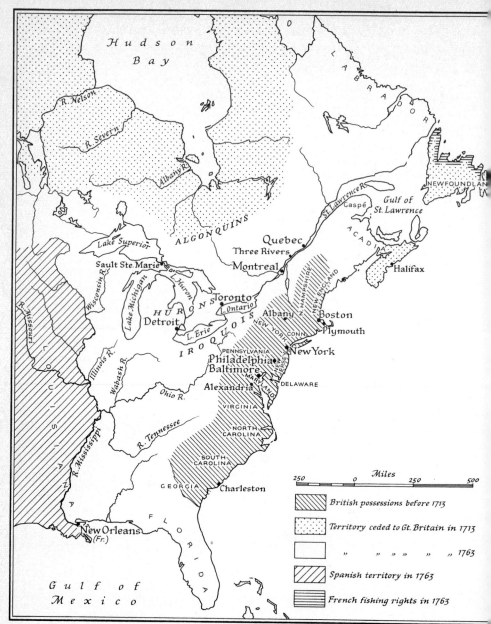

116 North America in 1763

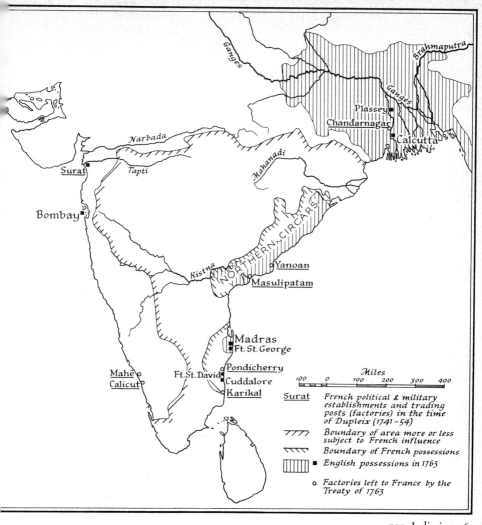

Miles

| 100 | 0 | 100 | 200 | 300 | 400 |

Surat     French political & military
         establishments and trading
         posts (factories) in the time
         of Dupleix (1741–54)

//////    Boundary of area more or less
         subject to French influence

\\\\\\    Boundary of French possessions

||||| ■   English possessions in 1763

o      Factories left to France by the
         Treaty of 1763

117   India in 1763

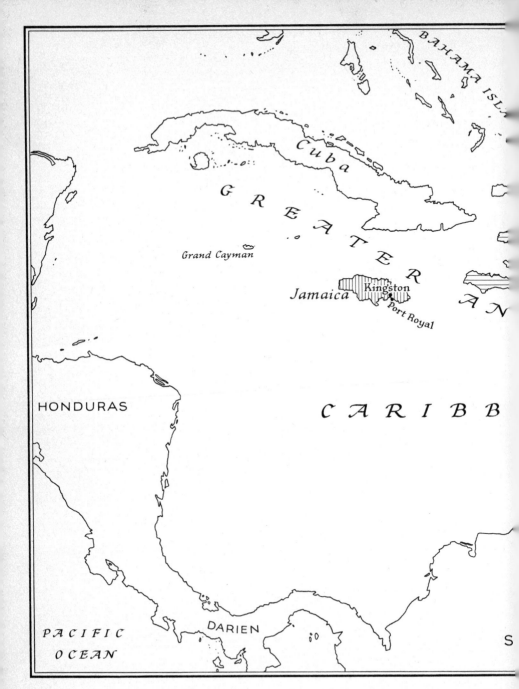

BAHAMA ISL

*Cuba*

G R E A T E R

A N

*Grand Cayman*

*Jamaica* Kingston

Port Royal

HONDURAS

C A R I B B

PACIFIC
OCEAN

DARIEN

S

Miles

100    0    100    200    300    400

(Br.)  British
(Sp.)  Spanish
(Fr.)  French
(Neu.)  Neutral
(Du.)  Dutch

Domingo

Puerto
Rico

*L E S S E R*

VIRGIN IS. (Br.)

Anquilla (Br.)
St. Bartholomew (Fr.)
Barbuda (Br.)

St. Eustatius (Du.)  St. Christopher (Br.)
Nevis        Antigua (Br.)

Montserrat (Br.)      La Désirade (Fr.)
Guadeloupe (Fr.)    Marie Galante (Fr.)

*LEEWARD
ISLANDS*

Dominica (Neu.)

Martinique (Fr.)

*N  S E A*

Ste. Lucia (Neu.)

St. Vincent (Neu.)
*WINDWARD
ISLANDS*                 Barbados (Br.)

Curacao (Du.)
Bonaire (Du.)

Grenada (Neu.)

Margarita (Sp.)

Tobago (Neu.)

Trinidad (Sp.)

*L L E S*

*A N T I L L E S*

I S H   M A I N

118 The West Indies in 1756

# NOTES

CHAPTER I
1 Quoted in Gomel, *Causes Financières de la Révolution Française* (Paris 1892), vol. I, p. 205, n. I
2 Arthur Young, *Travels in France*, ed. Maxwell (Cambridge 1929), p. 117
3 Quoted in A.M.Wilson, *Diderot* (New York 1957), p. 94
4 J.Flammermont, *Le Chancelier Maupeou et les Parlements* (Paris 1883), p. 636
5 Comte de Ségur, *Mémoires* (Paris 1825), pp. 19–20
6 *Ibid.*, p. 25
7 R.R.Palmer, *The Age of the Democratic Revolution* (Princeton 1959), vol. I, p. 4
8 *Parliamentary History*, vol. XV, p. 1269
9 *Mémoires de Frédéric II*, ed. Boutaric et Compardon (Paris 1866), p. 10

CHAPTER II
1 C.E.Labrousse, *La Crise de l'Economie Française* (Paris 1943), vol. I, p. 15
2 Quoted in Z.E.Rashed, *The Peace of Paris, 1763* (Liverpool 1951), p. 105
3 Charles Wilson, *England's Apprenticeship* (London 1965), p. 143
4 Turgot, *Oeuvres*, ed. Schelle (Paris 1913–23), vol. V, p. 168
5 Young, *op. cit.*, p. 173
6 *François Quesnay et la Physiocratie* (Institut National d'Études Démographiques, Paris 1958), vol. II, p. 537
7 Quoted in Robert Mauzi, *L'idée du Bonheur au XVIIIe Siècle* (Paris 1960), p. 156
8 Quoted in Georges Lefebvre, *La Grande Peur de 1789* (Paris 1932), p. 9
9 Quesnay, *op. cit.*, vol. II, p. 973
10 'Privilège', *Encyclopédie Méthodique Jurisprudence* (Paris 1786)
11 P.C.Yorke, *Life and Correspondence of Philip Yorke, Earl of Hardwicke* (Cambridge 1913), vol. II, p. 173
12 G.T.Matthews, *The Royal General Farms in Eighteenth Century France* (New York 1958), p. 111
13 M.Bloch, *Feudal Society* (London 1961), p. 336
14 *Lettre Adressée au Roi, par M. de Calonne* (London 1789), p. 126

15 Quoted in H. Sée, *Là France Economique et Sociale* (4th ed., Paris 1946), p. 87
16 H.Carré, *La Noblesse de France et l'Opinion Publique au XVIIIe Siècle* (Paris 1920), p. 126
17 Young, *op. cit.*, p. 265
18 Horace Walpole, *Letters*, ed. Mrs Paget Toynbee (Oxford 1903–25), vols. V and VI, p. 352
19 Charles Pinot Duclos, *Considérations sur les Mœurs*, ed. F.C.Green (Cambridge 1939), p. 127
20 *Ibid.*, p. 124
21 Sénac de Meilhan, *Considérations sur les Richesses et le Luxe* (Paris 1787), p. 89
22 Sénac de Meilhan, *Des Principes et Causes de la Révolution en France* (London 1790), p. 32
23 Turgot, *op. cit.*, vol. V, p. 188
24 Custine, *La Russie en 1839* (Paris 1843), vol. I, p. 143
25 Montesquieu, *De l'Esprit des Lois*, Book IV, ch. II
26 *Briefe eines schlesischen Grafen an einen kurländischen Edelmann* (Altona 1795), pp. 63, 99
27 Bossuet, 'Politique Tirée des Propres Paroles de l'Ecriture Sainte', in H.Bremond, *Textes choisis et commentés* (Paris 1913), vol. II, p. 122
28 *Ibid.*, p. 115
29 *Ibid.*, p. 111
30 Voltaire, *Siècle de Louis XIV*, ed. R.Groos (Paris 1947), p. 4
31 Marion, *Dictionnaire des Institutions de la France aux XVIIe et XVIIIe Siècles* (Paris 1923), 'Loi Salique'
32 P.Viollet, *Le Roi et ses Ministres* (Paris 1912), p. 527
33 H.Freville, *L'Intendance de la Bretagne, 1689–1790* (Rennes 1953), vol. I, p. 63
34 Quoted in Viollet, *op. cit.*, p. 549
35 Montesquieu, *op. cit.*, Book III, ch. X
36 H.Rosenberg, *Bureaucracy, Aristocracy and Autocracy. The Prussian Experience, 1660–1815* (Cambridge, Mass. 1958), p. 100
37 H.C.Foxcroft, *Life and Letters of George Savile, First Marquess of Halifax* (London 1898), vol. II, p. 497

38 Voltaire, *L'ingénu*, ed. Brumfitt and Davis (Oxford 1960), p. 38
39 Foxcroft, *op. cit.*, vol. II, p. 490
40 R. Saint-Étienne, 'Considérations sur les intérêts du Tiers-État' (in *Précis de l'Histoire de la Révolution Française*, ed. Boissy d'Anglas, Paris 1827), p. 6
41 Quoted in Viollet, *op. cit.*, p. 210
42 Rosenberg, *op. cit.*, p. 173
43 Quoted in Naudé, *Acta Borussica, Getreidehandelspolitik* (Berlin 1910), vol. III, p. 39
44 Quoted in Viollet, *op. cit.*, p. 259
45 Freiherr von Stein, *Briefe und ämtliche Schriften*, ed. Hubatsch (Stuttgart 1959), vol. II (i), pp. 209, 212
46 Quoted in P. Champion, *La France d'après les Cahiers de 1789* (4th ed., Paris 1911), p. 30
47 *Ibid.*, p. 29

CHAPTER III
1 Besenval, *Mémoires*, ed. Ségur (Paris 1805), p. 130
2 Condorcet, *Esquisse d'un Tableau Historique des Progrès de l'Esprit Humain*, ed. O. H. Prior (Paris 1933), p. 159
3 *Ibidem*
4 Montesquieu, *op. cit.*, Book XII, ch. I
5 D. Mornet, *Les Origines Intellectuelles de la Révolution Française* (5th ed., Paris 1954), p. 95
6 Ségur, *op. cit.*, p. 172
7 Walpole, *op. cit.*, pp. 334–5
8 Turgot, *op. cit.*, vol. V, p. 188
9 Bolingbroke, *Defence of the Treaty of Utrecht*, ed. G. M. Trevelyan (Cambridge 1932), p. 52

10 Quoted in A. M. Wilson, *French Foreign Policy during the Administration of Cardinal Fleury* (Cambridge, Mass. 1936), p. 292
11 *Mémoires de Frédéric II*, *op. cit.*, p. 69
12 Quoted in H. Dodwell, *Dupleix and Clive* (London 1920), p. 78
13 Francis Parkman, *France and England in North America*, selections by S. E. Morison (London 1954), p. 268
14 Quoted in H. Doniol, *Histoire de la Participation de la France a l'Établissement des États-Unis d'Amérique* (Paris 1886–92), vol. I, pp. 2–3

CHAPTER IV
1 Martin Göhring, 'Die Ämterkäuflichkeit im Ancien Régime', *Historische Studien* (Berlin 1938), p. 147
2 *Lettre adressée au Roi*, p. 70
3 Calonne, *Speech to the Assembly of Notables* (English tr., London 1787), pp. 29 ff.
4 J. F. Bosher, *The Single Duty Project* (London 1964), p. 14
5 House of Commons 78, vol. XIV, p. 501
6 Quoted in Marc Bloch, 'La Lutte pour l'Individualisme Agraire', *Annales d' Histoire Economique et Sociale* (Paris 1930), p. 381
7 *Ibid.*, p. 354
8 *Ibid.*, p. 512
9 *Ibid.*, p. 524
10 *Ibid.*, p. 542
11 *Lettre adressée au Roi*, p. 67
12 Saint-Étienne, *op. cit.*, p. 50

Readers wishing to acquaint themselves further with the meanings of these and other technical or obsolete terms will find a useful starting-point in Marion's *Dictionnaire des Institutions de France aux XVII^e et XVIII^e siècles* (Paris 1923). The explanations given below do not aim at being comprehensive but merely attempt to provide as much information as has seemed necessary to an understanding of the text.

BOURGEOIS (*see also under* NOBLES)
The meaning of this term was hardly clearer in the eighteenth century than it is today. In one of its eighteenth-century usages it referred to a legal category – i.e., to people who had lived in a town for a specified period, who, in many towns, were also required to own urban property and pay municipal taxes, and who were entitled to special privileges. In the phrase 'Bourgeois de Paris', for example, *bourgeois* is to be understood in this sense.

In the eighteenth century, however, people were commonly described as *bourgeois* not because of their legal status but because of their professions, behaviour or attitudes of mind. Under the Ancien Régime the members of military families, for example, often referred to the Nobles of the Robe (q.v.) as *bourgeois* even though many of these nobles (Turgot and Malesherbes, to mention only two cases) were of old and distinguished lineage with relations who had married dukes.

The criteria, in fact, which were used to distinguish the *bourgeois* from the nobleman were so numerous, so different and often (by modern standards) so absurd that it would need a Proust to do justice to them. The same difficulties beset the attempt to distinguish on the margins between the *bourgeois* and other members of the third estate.

On the other hand, in many connections it is reasonable to use the term *bourgeois*, as the present writer has generally used it in this essay, to mean people who neither belonged to the estate of the nobility on the one hand nor were peasants or urban workers on the other.

CAHIERS (DE DOLÉANCES)
The list of grievances customarily drawn up by each of the three orders or estates for presentation to the States General (q.v.).

CONTRÔLEUR GÉNÉRAL (DES FINANCES)
The holder of this post, the most important in the government, was in charge not only of the whole financial administration of the country, but also of agriculture, commerce, industry and communications.

## CORVÉE

A term principally applied in eighteenth-century France to the compulsory, unpaid labour on the roads introduced in the 1730s. Only *roturiers* (q.v.) were subject to this duty. The government justified its imposition on the grounds that it would fall on peasants at times of the year when they had no agricultural work and that this was preferable to imposing a tax on them, which they could not afford, from the proceeds of which the roads could be built with paid labour. As Turgot continually insisted, this argument was invalid. The *corvée* took men and animals from work on the land. It was felt to be an intolerable burden. It was also shown to involve an extremely wasteful use of resources because of the difficulties of assembling, training and disciplining a recalcitrant labour-force. The *corvée* continued in many parts of France up to the Revolution because of the difficulty of imposing the additional taxation necessary if the work were to be done by paid labour.

## GENERAL FARMERS (FERMIERS GÉNÉRAUX)

A company of financiers who under the Ancien Régime numbered between forty and sixty, and who, at six yearly intervals, concluded an agreement with the Crown known as the lease or 'bail'. The terms of the agreement obliged the company to pay the Crown a specified advance, or 'bonds-money', and a specified sum annually. In return, the company was granted the right to collect the indirect taxes and the income from the royal domain, and to manage the royal monopolies (particularly the salt and tobacco monopolies). In spite of the objections to it, the Farm proved indispensable to the Crown up to the Revolution because of the long-term loans which the General Farmers provided by means of the bonds-money, and the short term loans which they raised from the public (by means of the so-called *billets de ferme*) on the strength of their credit.

## INTENDANTS (DE PROVINCE)

The royal representatives in the provinces whose power over the population and other local authorities was virtually unlimited in law though (see p. 101) often by no means so in fact.

## LETTRES DE CACHET

Orders signed by the king and countersigned by a secretary of state, relating to an individual or to a particular case. Notorious as the instrument by means of which people were imprisoned without cause shown and kept in prison indefinitely without trial.

## NOBLE (*see also under* BOURGEOIS)

Legally, a noble was a person who enjoyed the privileges which belonged to all members of the second estate as such, for example, the right to carry a sword, to be tried by a special tribunal if he committed a criminal offence, to be exempt from the *Taille*, the *corvée*, etc. Families were ennobled in the following ways:

(1) by royal grant (given in return for money or other services, or because of an office which conferred nobility).

(2) by virtue of a title dating back to 1400 (*noblesse chevaleresque*) or to 1500 (*noblesse d'ancienne extraction*) for which no royal grant could be proved.

Even from the purely legal point of view, however, there were awkward cases: for example, the people who held offices conferring nobility that remained personal as distinct from hereditary until certain conditions were fulfilled (e.g., until the office had been held for twenty-five years). In 1789 nobles in this category were not allowed to vote with the order of the nobility in the elections to the States General.

From every point of view other than the purely legal one, the problem of what constituted the noble presented the same difficulties as did the allied problem of what constituted the *bourgeois*.

## ORDERS OR ESTATES

Categories of people (not to be confused with social classes) who supposedly fulfilled particular functions by means of a hierarchy rank, and who were distinguished by particular rights, or privileges, enforceable at law. In France these orders or estates were the first order or estate of the Church, the second order or estate of nobility, and the third estate – i.e., everyone not a nobleman or a churchman. Estates in this sense are not to be confused with Estates in the sense of provincial estates (see *Pays d'Etats*) or the Estates or States General (q.v.).

## PARLEMENTS

The Parlements were not parliaments in the modern sense of the word since their members were not elected but bought their offices, and since their principal function was the administration of justice. In 1789 there were thirteen Parlements – the Parlements of Paris, Toulouse, Grenoble, Bordeaux, Dijon, Rouen, Aix, Rennes, Pau, Metz, Besançon, Douai and Nancy. Each was the highest court of justice in its area. Besides their judicial functions, the Parlements exercised wide powers of police and administration and acquired great political power by virtue of the fact that royal edicts did not have the force of law in any area unless registered by the Parlement concerned.

## PAYS D'ETATS

Provinces in which local Estates survived until 1789. In general, though Languedoc was a notable exception, these were provinces (e.g., Burgundy, Brittany, Béarn, Navarre) which had been united to the French Crown at a relatively late date. The Estates were nominally assemblies of the three orders or estates (q.v.) of the province, meeting at regular intervals. In fact they were usually oligarchies dominated by the local nobility, or a section of it, with no claim to be called representative. They were endowed with certain administrative and political powers, particularly in matters of taxation. For example, they were responsible for levying themselves the direct taxes which in the rest of France were collected by royal officials, and they often succeeded in compounding their obligations for a lump sum. By these and other means they managed to escape with a much lighter tax burden than the other provinces. In consequence they were an object of suspicion to the Crown, which nevertheless did not dare to circumscribe their powers because of the uproar, and the charges of despotic action, which the attempt to do so always provoked. Further, the Estates raised loans for the Crown on the strength of their credit, and thus supplied the treasury with resources it could not afford to forego.

## PHILOSOPHE

In the eighteenth century, philosophy meant the secular study of the world and mankind, and thus included many subjects, for example the natural sciences, no longer associated with the term. The Philosophes – the name given to the leaders of the French Enlightenment and their apostles – thus saw all knowledge as their province. They nevertheless, as Condorcet said (see p. 123), believed that their principal function was not the pursuit of knowledge for its own sake but the education of public opinion.

## PHYSIOCRATS

A school, or, as it was often described at the time, a 'sect' of economists, sometimes called the 'Philosophes économistes'. Its leader was François Quesnay, doctor to Louis XV and Madame de Pompadour, whose works first attracted attention with the appearance, in the *Encyclopaedia*, of his articles 'Fermiers' (1756) and 'Grains' (1757), and with the publication of his famous *Tableau Economique* in 1758. The Physiocrats have been described as the first scientific school of political economy. Adam Smith, whom they greatly influenced, said of them that their 'system, with all its imperfections, is perhaps the nearest approximation to truth that has yet been published on the subject'. The Physiocrats based their doctrine on the assumption that all wealth was derived from land. From this assumption they deduced the conclusions, among others, that internal and external trade should be completely freed from all duties and other forms of government control, and that the existing taxes should be replaced by a single tax on land – the so-called 'impôt unique' which Voltaire once described as the 'impôt inique'. Notorious for the doctrinaire manner in which they expounded their theories, and for the absurdity of some of them, they provoked an impassioned opposition. Many of their ideas, nevertheless, particularly the importance they attached to agriculture, to increasing productivity, and to considering economic problems in the light of reason as distinct from custom, were generally accepted in enlightened circles, both in France and elsewhere.

## PRIVILÈGE

A term employed before the ideas of the Enlightenment gained general currency to mean the special rights conferred by law on particular groups or individuals (see particularly p. 46). As is explained on p. 54, *privilèges* in this sense could be either 'useful', i.e., confer a material benefit, or 'honorific', i.e., confer prestige. In the phraseology of the Enlightenment *privilège* commonly meant any advantage, but particularly money, which a person had not earned by his own legitimate efforts.

### ROBE. NOBLESSE DE ROBE

These terms were often used at the time, and have been used since, in vague senses. It has been claimed that the term 'la robe' should be understood to mean merely the people engaged in the administration of justice, many of whom were not nobles. The term 'noblesse de robe' seems most generally to have been used to mean the nobles employed in the royal administration, and has been so used in this essay. It excludes the ministers unless (as was commonly the case) they had begun their careers in the Parlements. It is a term denoting function, not social status (see pp. 66–7).

### ROTURIER

A member of the third estate (see under Orders or Estates).

### SEIGNEURIE. SEIGNEUR

The *seigneurie* (or, to give the nearest English equivalent, the manor) normally consisted of two different kinds of property of which the second was its distinguishing feature. In the terminology of the Ancien Régime these two kinds of property were the *domaine proche* or *direct*, and the *domaine utile* or *mouvance*. The *domaine proche* or *direct* was an area of land of which the *seigneur* usually cultivated a part for his own use with paid labour and let out the rest to tenant farmers or sharecroppers. The *domaine utile* or *mouvance* was an area inhabited by so-called peasant proprietors (see p. 38) who were required to render to the *seigneur* those payments and services known as 'feudal dues' (see pp. 39–40). Since the *seigneurie* had existed before the appearance of specifically feudal institutions, and also outlasted them, it is often maintained that these dues should properly be described as seigneurial and not feudal.

The *seigneur* was not necessarily a noble. Long before the eighteenth century *bourgeois* had bought *seigneuries*. Nor was the noble necessarily a *seigneur*, though if he were not, his aim was always to become one, since this title was prized more highly than any other below that of *Duc et pair*.

### SERFDOM

An institution which by the middle of the eighteenth century had largely disappeared in Europe west of the Elbe and north of the Danube but which persisted, notably, in Poland, Russia, the hereditary lands of the House of Habsburg and the territories of the Hohenzollerns east of the Elbe. Its distinguishing characteristics were that the peasants, as it was said, were 'tied to the soil'. They might not leave the estate, or marry, or engage in any occupation without the landlord's consent.

The landlord was at liberty to demand their labour without payment. They were forced to give their children into service in his household. In Russia the serfs had no rights in law and were subject to the landlord's jurisdiction in all matters without appeal. He might sell them not only with the estate but individually and apart from their families. In Prussia and the hereditary lands of the House of Habsburg the law allowed the serfs certain rights. These, however, for lack of machinery to enforce them, seem, for the greater part, to have been commonly not observed.

### SERVITUDES COLLECTIVES
The customary obligations, necessary to the working of the open-field system, enforced by the village communities on all cultivators of land, whether noble or *roturier*. They included, particularly, the obligation to sow the same crops as one's neighbours and to leave a proportion of one's land fallow. Their obverse were the communal rights, particularly the right to *vaine pâture* (q.v.).

### SHARE-CROPPING (MÉTAYAGE)
A system of land-tenure under which the landlord provides the implements and the seed in return for a proportion of the crop.

### STATES GENERAL (ETATS GÉNÉRAUX)
The French national assembly, consisting of representatives of the three orders or estates (q.v.). These estates elected their deputies and drew up their *cahiers* (q.v.) separately. They also debated separately after the States General had assembled. The last meeting of the States General before 1789 was in 1614.

### TAILLE
A tax levied only on commoners (*roturiers*, q.v.) or 'common' land (*terre roturière*). In practice it fell almost entirely on the peasants because of the exemptions granted to the towns as well as to the members of the first two estates. In the so-called *pays de taille personnelle* (the greater part of France), the *Taille* was levied on all the peasants' possessions at the arbitrary discretion of the collectors. Elsewhere (in the so-called *pays de taille réelle*) it was levied only on 'common' land. In the *pays de taille personnelle* the personal possessions of the nobleman were exempt, as was also the land he cultivated with paid labour, up to an extent that varied from one part of France to another but was commonly the area that could be ploughed with four ploughs. The land, however (usually the bulk), that he let out to tenants, was subject to the *Taille* which the tenants passed on to him wholly or partially. In the *pays de taille réelle* the landlord's tenants, and he himself, paid the *Taille* on any 'common' land in their possession.

The *Taille* provided overwhelmingly the greater part of the sums levied in direct taxation under the Ancien Régime.

## Vaine Pâture

The right of the inhabitants of the village, both noble and *roturier*, to pasture their beasts on the common lands, which included the open fields after the harvest, the meadows after the first hay harvest and the fields left fallow. The most intractable of the obstacles in the way of enclosures which were the *sine qua non* of agricultural improvement.

## Vingtième

A permanent tax, mainly on income from land, first imposed by Machault d'Arnouville in 1749 and falling on all landholders regardless of status. It was designed both to subject to direct taxation such parts of the nobleman's landed income (including his income from feudal dues) as had hitherto been exempt, and to provide a better means of taxation than the *Taille* (q.v.). Originally intended to yield 1/20th of all incomes from land, it was subsequently increased to 1/10th and then to 3/20th, and was further augmented by various 'sous pour livre', i.e., an increase of 5 per cent or more on the sums payable. Highly sophisticated attempts were made to ensure that this tax should not be arbitrary. It was hoped that ultimately it would supplant the *Taille* and thus subject all French landholders to equality before the law in matters of taxation. These attempts, however, failed because of administrative difficulties, and because the government's need for money was always so pressing that it could never afford to incur the short-term losses that a diminution, let alone abandonment, of the *Taille* would have entailed, for the benefits of the long-term gains which a more rational tax system would have brought.

# BIBLIOGRAPHY

Readers wanting a detailed bibliography for the period of European history covered by this essay should consult E. Préclin and V.-L. Tapié, *Le XVIII<sup>e</sup> Siècle*, 2 vols (Paris 1952) in the 'Clio' series, and J. Godechot, *Les Révolutions 1770–1779* (Paris 1963) in the 'nouvelle Clio' series. M. S. Anderson gives a list of the principal general works and text books in Appendix I of his *Europe in the Eighteenth Century* (London 1961). The works listed below are those to which the present writer is particularly indebted, or believes will be particularly helpful to readers wishing to pursue in more detail the themes discussed in this essay.

## FRENCH PEASANTS AND THE FRENCH ECONOMY

M. Bloch     *Les Caractères Originaux de l'Histoire Rurale Française* (3rd edition, Paris 1960)
'La Lutte pour l'Individualisme Agraire' (*Annales d'Histoire Economique et Sociale*, vol. 2, Paris 1930)

C. E. Labrousse     *La Crise de l'Economie Française à la Fin de l'Ancien Régime et au Début de la Révolution* (Paris 1943)

G. Lefebvre     *La Grande Peur de 1789* (Paris 1932)
*Études sur la Révolution Française* (Paris 1954)
*Études Orléanaises*, vol. 1 (Paris 1962)

P. de Saint Jacob     *Les Paysans de la Bourgogne du Nord au Dernier Siècle de l'Ancien Régime* (Paris 1960), Chapters II to VI

H. Sée     *La France Économique et Sociale* (Paris 1946)

## THE PEASANT PROBLEM IN CENTRAL AND EASTERN EUROPE

### HEREDITARY LANDS OF THE HOUSE OF HABSBURG

J. Blum     *Noble Landowners and Agriculture in Austria, 1815–1848* (Johns Hopkins University Studies, vol. LXV, Baltimore 1948)

C. Grünberg     *Die Bauernbefreiung und die Auflösung des gutsherrlich-bäuerlichen Verhältnissen in Böhmen, Mähren und Schlesien*, 2 vols. (Leipzig 1893–94)

P. I. Mitrofanov     *Joseph II. Seine politische und kulturelle Tätigkeit*, 2 vols., translated from the Russian by V. von Demelič (Vienna 1910)

PRUSSIA
O. Hintze  Zur Agrarpolitik Friedrichs des Grossen (*Forschungen zur brandenburgischen Geschichte*, vol. x, Berlin 1898)
G. F. Knapp  *Die Bauernbefreiung und der Ursprung der Landarbeiter in den älteren Theilen Preussens*, 2 vols. (Munich 1927)

RUSSIA
J. Blum  *Lord and Peasant in Russia from the Ninth to the Nineteenth Century* (Princeton 1961)
M. Confino  *Domaines et Seigneurs en Russie vers la fin du XVIIIᵉ Siècle* (Paris 1963)

## NOBLES AND BOURGEOIS

FRANCE
T. F. Bluche  *Les Magistrats du Parlement de Paris au XVIIIᵉ Siècle* (Paris 1960)
H. Carré  *La Noblesse de France et l'Opinion Publique au XVIIIᵉ Siècle* (Paris 1920)
A. Daumard and  *Structures et Relations Sociales à Paris au XVIIIᵉ Siècle* (Cahiers
F. Furet  des Annales, 18, Paris 1961)
F. L. Ford  *Robe and Sword* (Harvard 1953)
R. Forster  *The Nobility of Toulouse in the Eighteenth Century* (Baltimore 1960)
P. Goubert  *Familles Marchandes sous l'Ancien Régime: Les Danse et les Motte de Beauvais* (Paris 1959)
  *Beauvais et le Beauvaisis* (Paris 1960)
G. Lefebvre  *Études Orléanaises* (Paris 1962)
A. de Tocqueville  *L'Ancien Régime et la Révolution*, ed. G. Lefebvre (Paris 1952)
G. Zeller  *Aspects de la Politique Française sous l'Ancien Régime* (Paris 1964). See particularly Chapter XVII, 'Une notion de caractère historico-social: la dérogeance'

*Contemporary works*
C. P. Duclos  *Considérations sur les Moeurs*, ed. F. C. Green (Cambridge 1939)
Comte de Ségur  *Mémoires* (Paris 1825)

PRUSSIA
H. Rosenberg  *Bureaucracy, Aristocracy and Autocracy: The Prussian Experience, 1660–1815* (Cambridge, Mass. 1958)

203

# TAXATION AND GOVERNMENT FINANCE IN FRANCE

B.Behrens  'Nobles, Privileges and Taxes in France at the end of the Ancien Régime' (*Economic History Review*, Second Series, vol. xv, no. 3, 1963)

J.F.Bosher  *The Single Duty Project* (London 1964)

C.Gomel  *Causes Financières de la Révolution Française*, 2 vols. (Paris 1892–3)

M.Marion  *Les Impôts Directs sous l'Ancien Régime* (Paris 1910)
  *Histoire Financière de la France*, vol. 1 (Paris 1927)

G.T.Matthews  *The Royal General Farms in Eighteenth Century France* (New York 1958)

# PRIVILEGE. SALE OF OFFICES.
# THE OPPOSITION OF THE PARLEMENTS

J.Egret  *La Pré-Révolution Française, 1787–1789* (Paris 1962)

J.Flammermont  *Le Chancelier Maupeou et les Parlements* (Paris 1883)

M.Göhring  'Die Ämterkäuflichkeit im Ancien Régime' (*Historische Studien*, Berlin 1938)

R.Mousnier  *La Vénalité des Offices sous Henri IV et Louis XIII* (Rouen 1945)

J.M.Olivier-Marton *L'Organisation Corporative de la France d'Ancien Régime* (Paris 1938)

*Contemporary works*

Debate between Turgot and Miromesnil on the abolition of the *corvée*, 1776, in Turgot *Oeuvres*, ed. Schelle (Paris 1913–23), vol. v, pp. 163 ff.

For other contemporary works on this subject, see below under *Growth of Revolutionary Thought*.

# THE ABSOLUTE MONARCHY

## FRANCE

G.Pagès  *La Monarchie d'Ancien Régime en France* (5th edition, Paris 1952)

R.Mousnier and  'Quelques Problèmes concernant la Monarchie Absolue' (in
F.Hartung  *Relazioni del X Congresso Internazionale di Scienze Storiche. Storia Moderna*, vol. iv, Florence 1955)

P.Viollet  *Le Roi et ses Ministres Pendant les Trois dernières Siècles de la Monarchie* (Paris 1912)

*Contemporary works*

Bossuet  'Politique Tirée des Propres Paroles de l'Ecriture Sainte' in H.Brémond, *Textes choisis et commentés*, vol. ii (Paris 1913)

Calonne  *Speech to the Assembly of Notables* (Eng. trans., London 1787)
  *Lettres Adressée au Roi* (London 1789)

| | |
|---|---|
| Montesquieu | *De l'Esprit des Lois* |
| Voltaire | *Le Siècle de Louis XIV*, ed. R. Groos (Paris 1947) |
| | *L'Ingénu*, ed. Brumfitt and Davis (Oxford 1960) |

PRUSSIA

| | |
|---|---|
| C. Hinrichs | *Preussen als historisches Problem* (Gesammelte Abhandlungen, ed. G. Oestreich, Berlin 1964) |
| W. L. Dorn | 'Prussian Bureaucracy in the Eighteenth Century' (in *Political Science Quarterly*, vols. 46 and 47 for 1931 and 1932) |
| O. Hintze | *Staat und Verfassung* (Gesammelte Abhandlungen, ed. G. Oestreich, Göttingen 1962) |

## THE NEW IDEOLOGY IN FRANCE

THE PHILOSOPHES

| | |
|---|---|
| E. Cassirer | *The Philosophy of the Enlightenment* (Princeton 1951) |
| P. Gay | *Voltaire's Politics* (Princeton 1959) |
| | *The Party of Humanity* (London 1964) |
| R. Mauzi | *L'Idée du Bonheur au XVIIIe Siècle* (Paris 1960) |
| D. Mornet | *Les Origines intellectuelles de la Révolution Française, 1715–1787,* |
| A. M. Wilson | *Diderot* (New York 1957) |

*Contemporary works*

| | |
|---|---|
| Condorcet | *Esquisse d'Un Tableau Historique des Progrès de l'Esprit Humain*, ed. O. H. Prior (Paris 1933). English translation by J. Barraclough, preface H. Hampshire (Library of Ideas, London 1955) |
| J. Lough | *The Encyclopédie of Diderot and D'Alembert* (Selected Articles, Cambridge 1954) |
| J.-J. Rousseau | *Discours sur l'Inégalité parmis les Hommes* |
| Voltaire | 'Dialogues entre A.B.C.' (in *Dialogues . . . Philosophiques*, ed. R. Naves, Paris 1955) |

THE PHYSIOCRATS

| | |
|---|---|
| H. Higgs | *The Physiocrats* (London 1897) |
| G. Weulersse | *Le Mouvement Physiocratique en France de 1756 à 1770* (Paris 1910) |
| | *La Physiocratie à la fin du Règne de Louis XV, 1770–1774* (Paris 1959) |
| | *La Physiocratie sous les Ministères de Turgot et de Necker, 1774–1781* (Paris 1950) |

*Contemporary works*

Quesnay, *Textes* (in vol. II of *François Quesnay et la Physiocratie*, published by the Institut National d'Études Demographiques, Paris 1958)

Turgot on the grain trade, in 'Projet de lettre au Contrôleur Général Bertin' (*Oeuvres*, ed. Schelle, vol. II, pp. 122 ff.)

*The Growth of Revolutionary Thought*

P. Bastide  *Sieyès et sa pensée* (Paris 1939)
B. Fäy  *L'Esprit Révolutionnaire en France et aux États Unis à la fin du XVIII$^e$ Siècle* (Paris 1925)

*Contemporary works*

Barnave  'Introduction à la Révolution Française' (*Oeuvres*, ed. M. Bérenger de Drome, vol. I, Paris 1843)
R. Saint-Étienne  'Considérations sur les intérêts du Tiers-État' (in *Précis de l'Histoire de la Révolution Français*, ed. Boissy d'Anglas, 1827)
Sieyès  *Qu'est-ce que le Tiers État?* (1789); *Essai sur les Privilèges* (1788)

## ANGLO-FRENCH RIVALRY

J. Corbett  *England in the Seven Years War* (London 1907)
A. M. Davies  *Clive of Plassey* (London 1939)
H. Dodwell  *Dupleix and Clive* (London 1920)
W. L. Dorn  *Competition for Empire, 1740–1763* (New York 1940)
G. S. Graham  *Empire of the North Atlantic* (London 1958)
P. Mackesy  *The War for America, 1775–1783* (London 1964)
R. Pares  *War and Trade in the West Indies, 1739–63* (Oxford 1936)
  *Colonial Blockade and Neutral Rights, 1739–1763* (Oxford 1938)
F. Parkman  *France and England in North America*, selections by S. E. Morison (London 1956)
J. H. Parry and P. M. Sherlock  *A Short History of the West Indies* (London 1956)
H. Richmond  *The Navy in the War of 1739–48*, 3 vols. (Cambridge 1920)
  *Statesmen and Seapower* (Oxford 1946)
R. Waddington  *Louis XV et le Renversement des Alliances* (Paris 1896)
  *La Guerre de Sept Ans. Histoire diplomatique et militaire*, 5 vols. (Paris 1899–1904)
J. M. Wrong  *The Rise and Fall of New France* (London 1928)

## ENLIGHTENED MINISTERS AND OFFICIALS

M. Bordes,  'Les Intendants éclairés à la fin de l'Ancien Régime' (*Revue d'Histoire Economique et Sociale*, vol. 39, Paris 1961)
D. Dakin  *Turgot and the Ancien Régime* (London 1939)
P. Grosclaude  *Malesherbes: Témoin et Interprète de son Temps* (Paris 1961)
P. Jolly  *Calonne* (Paris 1949)
R. Lacour-Gayet  *Calonne* (Paris 1963)
M. Marion  *Machault d'Arnouville* (Paris 1891)

# LIST OF ILLUSTRATIONS

207

29 Emmanuel-Joseph Sieyès (1748–1836). Anon. caricature. Bibliothèque Nationale

30 The port of Bordeaux. Painting by Claude-Joseph Vernet; 1759. Musée de la Marine, Paris. Photo: Bulloz

31 Château de Pinsaguel. Photo: Studio Yan

32 *Tabatière* of the Duc de Choiseul, with miniatures by Louis-Nicolas (van) Blarenberghe; about 1770. Collection of the Baronne Elie de Rothschild. Photo: Bulloz

33 Marquis de Maillebois (1682–1762). Anon. painted portrait. Musée de Versailles. Photo: Réunion des Musées Nationaux

34 Duc de Belleisle (1684–1761). Copy in oils of a pastel by Maurice-Quentin de la Tour. Municipalité de Metz

35 *Renaud dans les jardins d'Armide.* Painting by J.H.Fragonard; about 1764. Collection: Veil-Picard, Paris

36 Performance of an *Opéra Comique* in the Salle de la Comédie Italienne in 1772. Sketch and watercolour by P.A.Wille. Bibliothèque de l'Opéra, Paris. Photo: Pic

37 Barnave (1761–93) at the Assemblée de Vizille. Sketch by Debelle. Bibliothèque de Grenoble. Photo: Picardy

38 C.Duclos (1704–72). Anon. painted portrait. Musée de Versailles. Photo: Réunion des Musées Nationaux

39 *Thé à l'anglaise chez la Princesse de Conti.* Painting by Michel-Barthélémy Ollivier; 1766. Louvre. Photo: Giraudon

40 *Fête à St-Cloud.* Painting by J.H.Fragonard; about 1775. Collection de la Banque de France, Paris

41 Hôtel Soubise, Paris. Interior by Boffrand; 1735. Plastic decoration by Harpin. Paintings by Natoire

42 Commode by Charles Cressent; about 1740. Wood, gilt bronze, inlaid with rosewood. Residenz, Munich

43 Sécrétaire by François Oeben; about 1760. Wood, ormolu, marble top; mounts by Charles Duplessis; inlaid with mahogany, rosewood, maple, boxwood, ebony and coloured woods. Residenz, Munich

44 *'Parade': invitation pour le spectacle des petits appartements de Mme de Pompadour.* Contemporary engraving by Charles-Nicolas Cochin. Bibliothèque Nationale

45 *Cavalcade du roi après le sacre de Louis XV à Rheims,* 26 October 1722. Painting by J.B. Martin. Musée de Versailles. Photo: Réunion des Musées Nationaux

46 Bossuet. Painted portrait by Hyacinthe Rigaud, jointly with Charles Sévin de la Pennaye; 1702. Louvre. Photo: Archives Photographiques

47 Louis XIV. Painted portrait by Hyacinthe Rigaud; 1701. Louvre

48 *The Pack.* Gobelins tapestry from the series 'Louis XV's Hunts' designed by J.B.Oudry; 1743. Uffizi, Florence

49 High-warp technique of tapestry manufacture. Plate from the *Encyclopaedia.* British Museum. Photo: Freeman

50 Louis XIV visiting the Gobelins factory. Gobelins tapestry designed by Charles Le Brun; about 1665. Gobelins Museum, Paris. Photo: Giraudon

51 Jeanne-Antoine, Marquise de Pompadour. Painting by François Boucher; mid-eighteenth century. Reproduced by permission of the Trustees of the Wallace Collection, London

52 Louis XV. Painting by Hyacinthe Rigaud; 1730. Musée de Versailles. Photo: Réunion des Musées Nationaux

53 Map of the route from Sens to Troyes in the period 1768–86. Watercolour. Musée de l'Histoire de France. Photo: Archives Nationales

54 Canals and Locks. Plate from the section *Hydraulique* of the *Encyclopaedia.* British Museum. Photo: Freeman

55 Map of the Intendance and Pays d'Etat of France, 1789. Drawn by Mrs P.S.Verity

56 Marquis de Tourny (1690–1760). Anon. pastel portrait. Musée du Périgord, Périgueux. Photo: Gauthier

57 Chaumont de la Galaizières. Engraved portrait by Christophe Guérin; 1781. Cabinet des Estampes, Strasbourg

58 François Daguesseau. Painted portrait by Robert Tournières; about 1717–22. Musée des Arts Décoratifs, Paris

59 Catherine II walking her dog at Tsarskoye Selo. Engraving after Borovikovsky; about 1794 (?). British Museum. Photo: Freeman

60 Frederick the Great. Engraved portrait after Daniel Chodowiecki. British Museum. Photo: Freeman

61 *Lettre de cachet* concerning Voltaire, 17 May 1717. Bibliothèque de l'Arsénal, Paris. Photo: Colomb-Gérard

62 Elevation of the Bastille. Watercolour drawing; 1750. Bibliothèque Nationale

63 Berryer. Painted portrait by J. F. Delyen; 1756. Musée de Troyes

64 Malesherbes (1721–94). Anon. painted portrait. Collection of the Comte de Tocqueville, Paris

65 The Empress Maria Theresa with her consort the Emperor Francis I and thirteen of her children. Miniature on paper after Martin van Mytens; 1760. Kunsthistorisches Museum, Vienna

66 Emperor Joseph II and his younger brother, Leopold II, Grand Duke of Tuscany, in Rome, 1769. Painting by Pompeo Batoni. Kunsthistorisches Museum, Vienna

67 Pierre-Victor, Baron de Bésenval (1722–94). Painted portrait by J. H. Nattier. Collection of the Prince de Broglie, Paris. Photo: Braun et Cie

68 Le Grand Condé (1621–86). Painted portrait by Juste d'Egmont. Château de Versailles. Photo: Giraudon

69 Le Maréchal de Soubise (1715–87). Anon. painted portrait. Archives Nationales, Paris. Photo: Eileen Tweedy

70 Le Maréchal de Saxe (1696–1750). Painted portrait by Maurice-Quentin de la Tour. Staatliche Kunstsammlungen, Dresden. Photo: Deutsche Fotothek, Dresden

71 Miromesnil. Marble bust by J. A. Houdon; after 1781. Musée Fabre, Montpellier

72 Château de Villette at Condécourt. Photo: Studio Yan

73 Condorcet (1743–94). Anon. painted portrait. Musée de Versailles. Photo: Réunion des Musées Nationaux

74 Denis Diderot. Bronze bust by Jean-Baptiste Pigalle; 1777. Louvre

75 D'Alembert. Pastel portrait by Maurice-Quentin de la Tour; 1753. Louvre. Photo: Archives Photographiques

76 Title-page of the first volume of the *Encyclopaedia*; 1751. British Museum. Photo: Freeman

77 Jean-Jacques Rousseau (1712–78). Painted portrait by Allan Ramsay. National Gallery of Scotland, Edinburgh

78 Skeleton. Plate from the section *Anatomie* of the *Encyclopaedia*. British Museum. Photo: Freeman

79 *M. et Mme Helvétius et leurs filles*. Watercolour by Carmontelle (Louis de Carrogis); 1760. Collection of the Comte d'Andlau. Photo: Bulloz

80 *La querelle entre Voltaire et Rousseau*. Anon. engraving; second half of the eighteenth century. Bibliothèque Nationale

81 Voltaire. Marble bust by J. A. Houdon; 1781. Collections de la Comédie Française. Photo: Jean Roubier

82 Baron Holbach. Painted portrait by Alexander Roslin; about 1770. Collection Daniel Wildenstein, New York. Photo: Les Beaux Arts, Paris

83 *Couronnement de Voltaire au Théâtre Français*, March 1778. Sketch in ink and watercolour by Gabriel de St-Aubin. Louvre. Photo: Archives Photographiques

84 *La famille Calas*. Watercolour by Carmontelle; 1762. David-Weill Collection, Paris. Photo: Courtauld Institute of Art, University of London

85 Necker (1732–1804). Painted portrait by J. S. Duplessis. Musée de Versailles. Photo: Réunion des Musées Nationaux

86 *Le rappel de Monsieur Necker*. Anon. engraving; 1788 (?). Bibliothèque Nationale

87 Turgot (1727–81). Painted portrait by Joseph Ducreux. Musée de Versailles. Photo: Réunion des Musées Nationaux

88 Colbert (1619–83). Detail of marble bust by Antoine Coysevox. Photo: Giraudon (Mansell Collection, London)

89 *Commerce des esclaves à Martinique.* Anon. eighteenth-century engraving. Bibliothèque Nationale

90 Château de Serrant. Photo: Jean Roubier

91 View of Louisbourg (detail). Anon. watercolour; about 1750. Map room, British Museum. Photo: Freeman

92 Joseph-François, Marquis Dupleix (1697–1764). Engraved portrait by Mme de Cernel after Sergent. Bibliothèque Nationale

93 Vaux-le-Vicomte, the façade and gardens. Photo: Giraudon

94 Nicolas Fouquet (1615–80). Painted portrait by Sebastien Bourdon. Musée de Versailles. Photo: Réunion des Musées Nationaux

95 Battle of the Plains of Abraham, 13 September 1759. Engraving by P.C.Canot after Capt. Hervey Symth. Courtesy of the Trustees, National Maritime Museum, Greenwich

96 Choiseul. Painted portrait by L.M. Van Loo; 1763. Musée de Versailles. Photo: Réunion des Musées Nationaux

97 Vergennes (1717–87). Pastel portrait by Gustaf Lundberg. Louvre. Photo: Archives Photographiques

98 Cut-away view of ship. Plate from J.G. Heck, *Iconographic Encyclopaedia*; 1851. British Museum. Photo: Freeman

99 French naval architects at work. Engraving by Ozanne from Duhamel du Monceau, *Traité de la construction pratique des vaisseaux*; 1758. British Museum. Photo: Freeman

100 Machault d'Arnouville (1701–94). Anon. painted portrait. Musée de Versailles. Photo: Réunion des Musées Nationaux

101 *Buffet de la cour.* Anon. caricature; 1787. Bibliothèque Nationale

102 *Assemblée des Notables presidée par Louis XVI en 1787.* Sketch in ink and watercolour by Moreau-le-jeune. Louvre. Photo: Giraudon

103 Calonne. Painted portrait by Elisabeth Vigée-Lebrun; 1784. Reproduced by gracious permission of Her Majesty the Queen

104 Loménie de Brienne (1724–94). Anon. painted portrait. British Museum. Photo: Freeman

105 Joly de Fleury. Engraving by R.Gaillard after Didier; 1780. British Museum. Photo: Freeman

106 Bertin (1719–92). Painted portrait by Alexander Roslin. Musée de Versailles. Photo: Réunion des Musées Nationaux

107 Queen Marie-Antoinette 'en Gaulle'. Painted portrait by Elisabeth Vigée-Lebrun; 1783. Wolfsgarten, Collection of S.K.H. Ludwig Prinz von Hessen und bei Rhein

108 Louis XVI. -Painted portrait by J.S. Duplessis; about 1780. Musée Rigaud, Perpignan

109 Hérault de Séchelles (1759–94). Anon. engraved portrait. Bibliothèque Nationale

110 A.J.M. Servan. Engraved portrait by L.A. Claessens; 1789 (?). Bibliothèque de Grenoble. Photo: Picardy

111 Le Peletier de St-Fargeau. Sketch by J.L. David; about 1790. Bibliothèque Nationale

112 Philippe-Egalité (1749–93). Painted portrait by Sir Joshua Reynolds. Musée Condé, Chantilly. Photo: Giraudon

113 *Monsieur Lucas au Palais-Royal.* Anon. caricature; 1789. Bibliothèque Nationale

114 Allegory on the Revolution. Painting by Jeaurat de Bertry; about 1789. Musée Carnavalet. Photo: Bulloz

115 Map of Europe about 1786. Drawn by Mrs P.S. Verity

116 North America in 1763. Drawn by Mrs P.S. Verity

117 India in 1763. Drawn by Mrs P.S. Verity

118 The West Indies in 1756. Drawn by Mrs P.S. Verity

Numbers in italics refer to illustrations